Critical Thinking in Young Minds

Victor Quinn

David Fulton Publishers

London

David Fulton Publishers Ltd
Ormond House, 26–27 Boswell Street, London WC1N 3JD

First published in Great Britain by David Fulton Publishers 1997

Note: The right of Victor Quinn to be identified as the author of this work has been asserted by him in accordance with the Copyright, Designs and Patents Act 1988.

Copyright © Victor Quinn 1997

British Library Cataloguing in Publication Data
A catalogue record for this book is available from the British Library

ISBN 1–85346–388–4

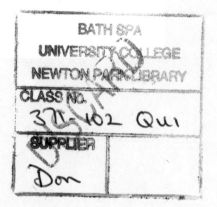
Typeset by Textype Typesetters, Cambridge
Printed in Great Britain by BPC Books and Journals, Exeter

Contents

Figures

Acknowledgements

I would like to thank the editors of *The Journal of Philosophy of Education*, and *If... then?: The Journal of Philosophical Enquiry in Education*, and S. Dingli (ed.), *Creative Thinking: A Multifaceted Approach*, University of Malta Press, for permission to use material first published there, which I have extensively developed. I am grateful too to R. J. Swartz and S. Parks for permission to use directly and to develop ideas from their book.

I am indebted to Bretton Hall College of Leeds University for a generous research-time allowance, to the Principal, Professor Gordon Bell, who constantly encouraged me after introducing me to David Fulton Publications, and to the College's Business Centre and research assistants for much help.

To a generation of Yorkshire children, of student teachers, of teachers in service, to my adopted school, North Featherstone J. I. and N. School, Wakefield, from which comes much of the transcript material, and to Throckley Middle School, Newcastle, which has adopted my practice and ideas in its development plan, I owe the sort of debt that makes this a book for my fellow teachers, more than one for my fellow academics and scholars.

To my adult children, Eugene, Jeremiah and Eithne, I owe the great debt of their guinea-pig status, since many of these ideas were first developed as I bathed them. Their critical-reading skills were also of great help. As always, my wife Trisha brought calm to 'critical' situations.

Media response to Victor Quinn's work

Alongside Victor Quinn's continuing academic work in the philosophy of education and critical thinking, his work in the classroom has delighted and challenged the media as much as it has children's minds. BBC and ITV viewers have seen seven- to thirteen-year-old children easing themselves into mastery of complex ideas and an overbearing authority figure. His work on moral education was used by the *Nine O'Clock News* (BBC) to contrast with Dr Nick Tate's 'Ten Commandments' approach.

Many journalists have watched him teach classes new to him. A pivotal moment in one of these is well caught by Brian James in the *Mail on Sunday*, subsequently reprinted in *Reader's Digest*:

> Victor Quinn stood glowering with pretend anger at the class of seven-year-olds at Yorkshire's North Featherstone J. and I. School. 'Look, I'm bigger than you, stronger and can shout louder. So if we have an argument I'll win. Won't I?'

> At the back of the class, Jodie rose. 'No, you won't win, 'cos you wouldn't be right.' Then, startlingly, 'There are two ways of winning.' A dozen children nodded in vigorous agreement . . .

> . . . Quinn deliberately escalated the row until it had reached the 'Oh yes he did, oh no he didn't' stage.

> Then he asked softly, 'Why is this silly?' – 'Because it could start a fight,' suggested a small boy.

> Then how could they go on? – 'I think,' said a voice, Jodie again, 'I'm not going to keep shouting back at you. I want to sit you down and talk to you and make you change your mind.'

In a lead feature in the *TES* (29 April 1994), Susan Young described a typical reaction of a deputy head to seeing the intellectual excitement of his class:

'I know these children very well – but when I see them with him I think I do underestimate them in many ways. It gives you an opportunity to look again.'

Victor Quinn has used video evidence of his work with Yorkshire and London children to show teachers at conferences across the world how easy it is to raise intellectual expectations.

PART A

Lesson plans and analyses

Chapter 1
Introduction

A book on critical thinking is difficult to write. I am forced to make assumptions about you (plural) which will be substantially wrong, since I don't know you. To deal with this, I think it best, in the introduction, to identify some of the assumptions I am making, and to match these assumptions with some of the ideas I am presenting, so that you can make of the book your own. In that way, you will decide what to ignore, what to start with and what to focus on.

What assumptions do I start with? The first is that you are dissatisfied with current practice in school, perhaps in your own classroom. Children often surprise us in the midst of routine activities by the profound question, by the glimpse of shocking intelligence, by the sheer intellectual care, or by the tenacious yet tender refusal to be browbeaten. This profundity, in the midst of our many cares, is something that frustratingly challenges us. We know that nurturing it is real education, we know that certain devices we have do facilitate it, without undue effort, and we wish we had a richer resource of such devices. My assumption is that you are at times a teacher with such needs: this book addresses them in a number of ways.

Before I detail the ways, I continue with the assumptions. My second is that you are somewhere along the line of focus in practice or focus in theory. I want to satisfy each focus, but I shall insistently root all points in practice, for two reasons. First, I want to change practice fundamentally; secondly, theory that is rooted in practice is a better thing, even as theory. It has usefully been said that good practice without theory is blind and good theory without practice is sterile. Forced to choose, I would opt for blindness, but I am not forced to choose, and I invite you, whatever your inclination, to strive for openness to the other side, to enrich your professionalism.

Along with theory come new words. Some people detest all jargon as a sign of insecurity and of mock professionalism. Others think nothing of a course or book that has not given them a range of new words to bandy about. My third assumption is that there are important concepts (whether new or old) supporting this work, and words derive their importance as means of handling these concepts. I will introduce a few uncommon words because they stand for powerful, transforming concepts and my case must rest, in your judgement, on whether you see these as either transforming or powerful.

My fourth and saddest assumption is that you are suffering, at whatever level you teach, from waves and layers of innovation, of fresh accountability and of pervasive pressure to 'deliver' 'results'. It is understandable that teachers facing such pressure shy away from an innovation that is not forced upon them, however much they value what it offers. I do not use the starting point that you are a quite free and eager agent, much as I would like to. Rather I will work at a level of reasonable beginnings, of enormous satisfactions, of the ways critical thinking can enhance NC work, and of ways in which it can make conspicuous to children, and to visitors to your classroom, that something very special is going on in this room in writing, in speaking and respectfully listening, in the nurture of intelligence and in the visual representation of ideas across your display and the curriculum.

I have to make assumptions about your levels of confidence, and these, like you, are diverse. Some of you are new to the area, wanting lessons well tried by me and others, to have a go at: I supply these. Some of you have experimented or worked extensively in the area, and come, maybe, with a distinct scepticism as to whether you can learn anything from me, and with a desire to prove me wrong. I hope that as both of 'you' try, read, suspect and continue experimenting, you will question your level of confidence. You may move either to a new confidence based on unexpected success, or to a new challenge about which you feel, despite your experience, distinctly up against your previous personal best. Whatever your level of confidence, I ask you not to allow yourself to be put off by mine. As I shall explain, my overbearing confidence is a challenge, an invitation to you, to develop a disagreement.

I assume that it is appropriate in this book to avoid an attempt to produce an academic text on the scholarship of critical thinking (CT) or on the state of CT in Britain or across the world.[1] By such a criterion, I would have failed. This is a personal book, based on personal experience and on personal reflection on that experience, addressing teachers. I strive for objectivity in that I check my claims against teachers' comments, video and transcript evidence and the regular observation of children's bodies and eyes after extended work. But I do not shun subjectivity in the sense that I am at the centre of this book, insisting time after time that the success of my work depends not on my personality but on skills, qualities and interactions that most teachers can learn. If you judge the book a failure, you will do so, I hope, on criteria that I avow, not on criteria that I disown.

My final assumption is about society, in part moulded by our schools. As teachers, we have betrayed generations of children in that we have produced tabloid fodder. Year after year our school-leavers become full members of society and yet they seem to bring no higher an expectation of autonomy to the minds of the mass-selling newspaper editors who seek sales, to the politicians who seek their vote, and the advertisers who seek their cash. They are not, year on year, more critical thinkers, more analytical, less gullible, nor, in my experience, are they more disposed to bring the force of reason and open-mindedness to their dealings with others, their decisions and actions. I point the finger at teachers, not because we alone might have influence, but because to the extent that we might have influence, we have largely not tried. Most school-leavers look blankly if asked what might be the ten most common unfair techniques of persuasion in a paper they read. Most of my graduate students look blankly if asked what might be the ten most common pejorative words used by politicians, to persuade unfairly. If they have not encountered these things in an educational context, it is not surprising that they have not developed immunity to them, not to say intolerance of them. It is intolerance that I seek.

So, put arrogantly, I want to interrupt the tabloid culture. I want children to delight in seeing the weakness of argument to which their parents are prey and victims. I want them to see the hypocrisy and contradiction which are endemic features of moral and political persuaders. I want them to be able to stand up to authority figures, teachers included, not with stubborn countersuggestibility, but with a respect for reason and argument in which all are invited to share.

Having stated my assumptions, I move to indicating the components I offer and the reasoning behind them, so that you can attend more intelligently to what you need. There is a mutually supportive, two-pronged approach, which might be defined as content and process.

The major component in content is a number of worked lessons for which I present a lesson plan and analysis. Without doubt, this will strike some readers as formulaic and too prescriptive. On the other hand, I know it is what some teachers want, and a begining from which they can grow into diversity. The worked lessons will have served little of their intended purpose if, however successful as one-offs, they do not come to be seen as generating new lesson ideas and as developing the generic features of what I am arguing. This would be the blindness of good practice without theory. In these chapters, however, I do intimate the generic features, skills, climate, etc, which I spell out in the process section.

The second component in content is an attempt to extend the range in less detail, over the curriculum, with ideas both for full lessons and for interventions within lessons. The precisely critical nature of the thinking in these will not be so evident, and will have to be derived from the more extensive treatments and from the process section. However, the sketches will permit a comprehensiveness, both of age range and of subject matter.

Process moves away from a subject or lesson focus, to a concern with the quality of pedagogy in any subject. Questioning is a strong example. An invitation to introduce or develop critical thinking is in good measure an invitation to develop your own and the children's questioning. The development involves both the kind of questions and the manner of asking. In videoing the moral lesson for this book, we recorded myself and the children talking at the end of the lesson about the different experience of being taught by me. I asked one nine-year-old boy in what way I was different. His reply was touching. He said that only once before had anyone asked him questions and really listened to the answers wanting to know what he thought and felt. 'That', he said, 'was the man from the council when me Mum and Dad were splitting up.' I reflected on the tragedy that it is only for therapy or diagnosis that real, interested questioning enters a child's life.

The second aspect of process is the rather posh-sounding 'intellectual virtues'. In a sense these are just ground-rules, upon which I am very strict. Even at their most 'ground-rulish', as with 'don't interrupt', they are undersold if they are thought of as conventions and not as part of the fabric of intellectual engagement. They exist to allow people to get the most out of each other's ideas, in giving and getting. The word 'virtues' is not out of place, for, though they are not moral qualities, they are qualities which we can similarly internalise and which place self-constraint upon us. Their scarcity, not just in the tabloid culture, but in the discussion of many adults and academics, is a further disquieting dimension of school and higher 'education'. A central term urged on your attention here is 'decentring'.

'Stop arguing!' children are told, at home and school. The advice is good, but badly worded. What is meant is usually that they should stop quarrelling, or arguing in such a way as to get nowhere in resolution, perhaps getting into a fight or building resentment and hate. Rather, what children should do is start arguing, knowing how. They should learn to identify the four kinds of argument, and the differently appropriate ways of attempting to resolve these. Having learned these (which may indeed be approached through a content lesson), they must learn to combine the new skills with the intellectual virtues so that the ego is tamed. Then the parental or teacher's advice is 'Start arguing', which they know to mean 'Stop quarrelling.'

Just as my readers are diverse, so are those they teach, and a major aspect of diversity that our culture has excluded is the visual organisation of ideas. In recent years, critical thinking has made huge strides to undo this injustice, and I shall introduce the use of graphic organisers and thinking maps as two powerful tools, not just for those who predominantly do visualise rather than verbalise, but for all of us, since these are more appropriate media for some conceptual material.

If there were only one idea whose importance I could guarantee you would take with you from this book, I would choose the distinction between the academic and the intellectual. OFSTED regularly confuses the two and calls them both 'academic'. The 'academic' refers to the conventions of a subject, its procedures and formal material; the 'intellectual' refers to the exercise of intelligence. Of course we want both, but I often see children faced with activities which have excessive expectations of them academically, whilst the intellectual expectations are laughably low.

Another regular observation is of children whose written (non-fiction) work leaves me despairing, in its inanity. I can have a wonderful visit to waste ground to collect interesting things, or a science or moral lesson in which they are orally speculating, proposing, planning, disagreeing in a profound way. They come to write about it and they are usually a great disappointment to themselves and me: their writing is no reflection of their previous critical thought. In a sense the answer to this, scribing, is obvious, though demanding of that most precious commodity, quality time. However, I have a number of suggestions, not only as to how the quality time can be used to generate more quality time, but as to how the already literate children can make a further breakthrough to literacy, to critical literacy. Further, the products can go on display – astonishing evidence of thoughtful writing – and also with children's accompanying analysis of the features that make it 'quality'. The analysis attends to features of syntax, of pragmatics, of paragraphing, etc, in such a way as to permit the children to develop models for their general non-fiction writing. I propose ways of infusing the quality of speech into their writing.

Children's thinking cannot take a great leap forward without their developing 'meta-thinking'. They must come to be not just thinkers, but thinkers about their own thinking. This allows them to register the features of quality thinking, to analyse the content and processes of their own thinking and to benefit from the reflexive perspective. In combination with appropriate humility and pride, it contributes richly to decentring.

Notes

1. I would be delighted if readers felt inclined to go on to more scholarly or academic books. Some recent ones are detailed in the bibliography. Michael Bonnett's book is a serious and penetrating examination of promoting understanding, looking at traditions of understanding. Bob Fisher's book *Teaching Children to Learn* introduces the reader to a wide range of recent literature and ideas, as well as drawing on his continuing classroom experience. Bob Ennis's book will develop and satisfy the interests generated in the application of informal logic to our thinking. Martin Coles and Will Robinson's book is a useful guide to recent programmes in teaching thinking. Undoubtedly, these thoroughly referenced books will develop confidence, perspective and future exploration, in addition to my intention of producing a book of ideas that succeeded along with ideas and practices that have made them succeed.

Chapter 2

Learning about contradictions

Introduction

This chapter develops a lesson as an instrument of powerful learning in critical thinking and in philosophy for children. It introduces a context for painlessly learning a narrative structure for a logical structure handled by all three-year-olds, and often badly by educated adults. And yet this structure is not attended to in standard schooling, to make the good handling out-weigh the bad. The structure is well enough learned, even in the first lesson, to allow below-average children to contribute to a deeply philosophical disagreement. With classes from eight-year-olds upwards, it has failed me only once, when not enough of the children were able to engage philosophically. We reverted then to taking the logical structure further, which is an educational aim well worth while, in its own right.

The structure of the chapter is to begin with a lesson plan. Ideally my reader would modify and try the lesson before reading further. After the plan I present brief extracts of video transcript from lessons I have taught to eight- to eleven-year-olds, with comments on each. I then suggest developments of the lesson in relation to the topic of critical thinking and relate them to the wider concerns of the book.

Lesson plan

Aims

- to develop sensitive and structured speaking and listening
- to develop peer-correction of structured thinking
- to gain delight in developing new understanding

- to enter new areas of intellectual interest
- to see further possibilities of the structure.

Introduction

With the class in a circle or facing front, indicate the novelty of the material and the concern with learning to think better. Stress the need for co-operation, no derision, and constructive agreement or disagreement. Mention, as a liberating factor, the absence of writing: i.e., 'work'.

Structured thought development

Establish the term 'contradiction', by giving a homely example: 'If I say the English team could never win, can you contradict me?' Present, say, three contradictions of the form: 'Once upon a time there was a universe in which there were no children, and a child there saw a fish in a stream.' Invite hands up on spotting a contradiction. When they are widely succeeding, ask them to invent a contradiction of the same form, but very simple: 'simple enough to teach contradictions to children two years younger than you'. Encourage peer agreement or articulation of disagreement with judgement, bringing the word 'contradiction' into the active vocabulary.

When this is done, offer more complex contradictions, of the same narrative/logical form, but with the crucial word not repeated, a narrative smoke-screen and more complex concepts, e.g., 'In a universe with no animals a pop star wore a pink shirt.' Endorse ambiguity of 'animal'. Now have children invent complex ones, leaving thinking time, and easing it for the less attuned by, at the end of the thinking time, giving massive help, e.g., 'In a universe with no water, a boy was thirsty after riding his bike, so since there was no water he had a drink of . . .', or '. . . he went for a swim in a . . .' Some ten-year-olds are at the stage of hands up for 'a boy': 'You couldn't have a human being without water.' Bright thirteen-year-olds will say that you couldn't in this universe, but you could in an imaginary one. The encouragement of such divergence and intelligence is a crucial part of the climate I am creating.

The concluding part of the lesson is the deep discussion. 'Here's one I don't know about. Once there was a universe without language, and in that universe, a girl and boy were walking alongside a river and the girl thought to herself . . .' (hands go up). I ask for explanation and have a vote. (There is usually overwhelming agreement that it is a contradiction.) I ask people to speak in favour of its being a contradiction, to encourage doubters. I ask for opposition, and the section conclusion is another vote. (The extent of mind-change is strongly age-dependent.)

The second section of the conclusion is continuing the story: '. . . she thought to herself that it was a pity there was no language so they could talk to each other.' (A sea of hands, even when I have tried it with educated adults.) Again a statement of the contradiction is sought and a vote taken. Many top juniors will not change their minds, but there will be argument about the possibility of thinking of things that do not exist, in this universe as well as in an imaginary one.

The lesson ends with a coming down to earth, acknowledging how deep the discussion has been and how well many have argued, attending to the widespread change of mind in response to reasons well given, and projecting as to how we might take it further.

Pedagogy

Changes of pace

Many teachers would be unhappy in contemplating a speaking and listening lesson as long as ninety minutes. If the diversity of the various sections of the lesson is psychologically used, if a growing sense of the power of what they are doing is communicated and if humour is used, I haven't found this a problem. But there are standard moves to avoid any problem.

'Buzz-groups' is probably the most useful move. In such a lesson, they serve a number of purposes. Psychologically they are a useful shift of attention from teacher-led to children-led exploration. They extend the range of spoken participation. They permit a more relaxed approach and the accompanying chance to ask about an earlier point missed, by a child not confident enough to ask in full class. In novel work like this, where many children get a greater sense of intellectual self-reliance and a stronger invitation than ever before to careful thinking, enormous intellectual energy is released and much thought is stored up in frustration. The buzz-group is sometimes introduced as open discussion time, sometimes with a particular brief: 'I want you all to talk and think of at least two things that have never existed but that we can imagine,' or 'See if each group agrees with Gemma's point that there's a difference between acorns and language, such that if neither existed, acorns could be imagined, but language could not.'

Buzz-groups help also with the reverse side of the intellectual riches story. I need regularly to be vigilant for the glazed faces of inattention. It is easy to allow the normal or new-found articulateness of half a dozen children to race ahead of the bewildered many. The group work allows that vital time to develop co-ordinates on a problem: to say, 'I don't get it,' or 'When Amy said . . . did she mean . . . ?' It allows the teacher to deal with the lost sheep.

Alongside group work is the pervasive need, not just for slower children, to slow things down. Hardly any children in most classes give enough time to thinking, or are encouraged to do so. With any activity demanding care, and critical thinking is just such, more time is needed. So the teacher is freer, and the pace is altered, by periodic slots, not to discuss, but to think alone. The question may be oral or on the board. Whichever, the introduction is an opportunity to remind the children of the qualities of thinking and discussion most in need of support.

Writing sentences in quoting children's ideas is a further diversity in the lesson. Such temporary display is more process than product display. It is not a waste of teaching time, but an opportunity to invite detailed attention to quality of thought, which is sometimes just as much attending to quality of language. As I shall argue later, quality non-fiction writing is extremely rare in primary schools. When the aspects of spoken thought enter the writing, whether by teacher- or peer-scribing, the poverty is changed utterly.

But whilst this is conceived as a speaking and listening lesson, I often do have a further contrast of activity by asking for a single sentence written, showing a contradiction of the simple sort. I do this not just for a change of action, but to identify, in a class new to me, anyone who is quite lost. It has the further advantage of reinforcing the narrative and logical structure so crucial both to the general critical thinking learning and to the complex items we move on to.

Many of the points that I have put are intended not just to allay the fears of teachers new to the approach but to achieve deeper purposes, as should be clear. This is equally true of my final point under pedagogy. One might feel out of one's depth dealing with the relationship between language and thought. On the one hand, that might be a reason to stop at the earlier stage, because already there, with enough practice, they have learned the fundamental relationship of universal claim and counter instance: to state both is a contradiction. But even there, one will often be presented with a suggestion not met before, and to which one does not know the answer. The get-out is subtle; it is more subtle than simply admitting ignorance. A central declaration is that the work is exploratory, not expository. Moreover, the central learning thrust is peer-correction; I see the teacher's role chiefly as insistence on quality of procedure. A good teacher is one who has learned forbearance. This does not mean that there are no right and wrong answers, but it is appropriate both to make explicit and to require that good argumentational procedure is more important than insisting on the correctness of one's view. This shift of emphasis is very easily stated but is by no means an easy option for many teachers, whose professional security is hugely bound up with being authorities on information, whose ability to forbear is still limited and whose awareness of intellectual virtue in discussion, with their peers or their classes, is sadly lacking.

So this last point, which started out as a reassurance to those worried about the limits of their own knowledge, may itself be an even greater source of worry: do they have the deep, alternative skills? To embrace critical thinking is to forgo the reassurance of familiar fact and to embrace the uncertainties and challenges of a dynamic pursuit of quality thinking, in the commonsense and uncommonsense world of children.

Transcript 1

The next three extracts are taken from a video of a group of four children from an ex-mining town in Yorkshire. I have taught these Year 6 children about eight times. The exchange is of the sort that would take place with a small group as I moved from group to group. Only Amy still believes there could not be thought in a universe without language.

A: If there were no language, how could she think to herself? What could she think if there were no language?

J: You could think of a picture of what you see.

G: You could think you had scored winning goal of the FA Cup, without saying words.

A: Yeah, but if you thought that, you wouldn't . . . like, how would they know how to score a goal; if there were no language? And because somebody would have to tell them how to score a goal, and if there were no language, how could they score a goal like that?

G: You don't need language to score.

A: You do.

G: You just kick ball.

VQ: Wait now, just a minute. When he said, 'You don't need language to score,' it doesn't help to say, 'You do.' Give him a reason. Give him a reason. Anyhow, let's leave you two there. What do you think, Richard? [who hasn't spoken yet].

R: I don't think there is a contradiction. You can think of anything and there doesn't have to be no language in what you are thinking. You can just think of an image.

In this exchange the general point is being advanced usefully by considering examples. These are closely accurate to purpose. Notice that Amy carefully does not confront Glen's obvious truth that language is not necessary in scoring, but rather in coaching or something wider. The procedural point is made, that simply disagreeing (as opposed to giving reasons) is not helpful. It might better be raised as a question, so that it is articulated by one of them. Look at Amy's longest contribution. Under pressure, her syntax is faltering. Her opening conditional statement collapses and gives way to a perfectly formed and economical conditional question, which shows the strength of logical grasp. See too the syntactic strength of her second (last) sentence: the 'And' is appropriate (other than to conservative pedants), the 'because' indicates a satisfied conditional, it is ranged alongside the stipulated conditional (no language), leading to the properly drawn question.

There is nothing remarkable in Amy's speech. It is the speech of any eleven-year-old placed in the same situation. Consider the value of this short piece of transcript to the children as they reprocess it to remove the false starts, to redraft it to their needs. The chief thing I would emphasise is the total contrast between this and their normal non-fiction writing, so lacking in connectives, in intellectual vigour, in personal commitment.

Richard's comment also rewards analysis. His opening denial of contradiction is as economical as it could be. He doesn't respond to the previous example, scoring goals, but to that of which it was an example. His second sentence uses the concept 'non-necessity', a vital concept, often badly handled by adults, as we shall see later. His final sentence gives a clear example, 'an image', of a non-contradiction, a not necessarily linguistic thought.

It might be useful to note the ideas presented by this group when all had agreed that thinking was possible in a language-free universe: scene, landscape, seascape, meta-thinking (I had introduced the term, since we were doing so much of it), glorious things, unhappy things, what you'll do when grown up, the future, people, the past, countries, dying or how you are going to die, your school, next.

Transcript 2

This video extract reveals the children rejecting the idea that one could think of language if it didn't exist. Again there is much in this that a teacher, or I, at any rate, would miss on first teaching it. The value of making transcripts is thus emphasised, if we are committed to improving our sensitivity to what is going on.

> VQ: Remember, put up your hand if you spot a contradiction: '. . . and the girl thought to herself that it was a pity there was no language in that universe so that they could speak to each other . . .' [all hands up] Amy, do you think that that is a contradiction?
>
> A: Yes, because if there was no language, 'pity' and all that (they are words), and if there were no language, she couldn't think it, if there were language. So she couldn't think!
>
> VQ: Yes, she couldn't think those words, you are right. But the question is could she think that thought?
>
> A: No.
>
> G: I have never had a thought of how to think how to have a picture of pity in your mind. It is a pity in your mind. We say, 'It is a pity,' but I have never had that picture.
>
> VQ: Right, just say that again.
>
> G: I have never had a picture that says, 'It's a pity.'

This is material rich in children thinking about thinking, in meta-thinking. But more importantly, it is rich in children developing strength in connectives. Amy's opening statement is a strong idea, twice affirmed, that can be reduced to 'No language, no thought', or to 'Language is a necessary condition of thinking.' Notice that the three 'if' clauses say the same thing, with the word 'no' left out of the third. Despite the repetition, there is a strong logical sense of the negative conditional and the negative consequence. In no way is this the outcome of teaching by me or anyone. It is picked up as most children learn certain language patterns. But often it is not picked up well enough for the more testing purposes to which it can, and usefully should, be put by children and adults.

Glen takes the idea forward in interesting ways. His point about never having had a picture of pity is also repeated, though to better purpose. The first statement contrasts thought and picture; the second contrasts saying and picturing. He avoids declaring the obvious relevance of this personal illustration to the topic, i.e., that it opposes the idea of thought without language. He also avoids saying, which would help the reader, that to this point the children have identified only pictures as possible language-free thoughts. Implicitly he is arguing that something has to be a picture for it to be entertained in a language-free universe.

My purposes in asking Glen to repeat what he said are complex. A major one is to allow an important point to register with others. Secondly, a restatement can helpfully reword: here it has the unexpected advantage of economising. It also helps to slow the process to a more reflective pace. The contrast with many classroom climates is that between a recollective and a reflective pace. I want Glen's point to be lingered over and fully appreciated.

Transcript 3

This transcript follows the two previous ones and shows the children thinking themselves away from their opening position.

VQ: Now try and think, in this universe, of things that do now exist that once didn't exist.

G: A television.

VQ: 'Television'. 'Once upon a time in this universe, there was no such thing as television.' Now was it possible for someone to think of television in that universe?

J: Yes, because there were language.

R: Yes, because someone did and they invented the television.

VQ: Let's take that again. Let's take that again. The question is, with regard to television, imagine this universe in which there is no such thing as television, and I said 'Is it possible in that universe to imagine a television?' and your answer is . . . ?

R: Yes, because someone invented one.

VQ: That is a very, very strong answer. If someone actually invented it then it is possible to invent it. But do you see that this is a difficulty for the story you presented me with [i.e., you couldn't imagine language in a language-free universe]?

I shall not elaborate here on points already made. One thing that is new here is my making the task of imagination easier. It is more difficult for eleven-year-olds to imagine the invention of language in this or an imagined universe than it is to imagine the invention of recent things in this universe. In bringing language in as the explanation of television's invention, I think Jody is misguided, though a complex case could be made. Ric's case is a powerful move, of great generality, and expressed with appropriate economy.

A further video transcript shows a much younger class at work. This is my first encounter with these eight-year-olds, in a small class of seventeen present, in a farming/dormitory village, more privileged than the previous children. At the point where the transcript starts, they have concluded that language is necessary for thought. So I ask them how then language started. They begin with biblical confidence, moving to cultural transition.

As I do not know the children's names, I use T for teacher and C for each child, apart from one girl, whom I call GC.

T: So where did language come from in the first place, if you have to have language in order to be able to think?

C: Yer Mam.

C: God.

T: God? Well, that's one . . . that's one account.

C: God taught the first person.

C: Adam.

T: Taught him . . . did he teach him English?

C: NO [emphatically], language.

C: Taught him LANGUAGE. And then . . . Adam taught . . . erm the people after him. And then . . .

C: I think . . . you've got to have a dead language.

C: And as time went on it turned into Roman language.

T: Sorry, did you say the dead language?

C: The dead language.

T: What's the dead language?

C: Latin. Nobody speaks it any more.

T: Oh yes. But it was once spoken. So where did Latin come from?

C: God. God taught Adam Latin. Adam taught other people.

T: Right. Right. OK?

GC: Eh, well do you know when you said you don't know where language comes from? Well people . . . the first person made it up by making different words: like that's called a 'book' [pointing]. They could have just said 'cul' or 'tar', something like that.

T: Ah! That's interesting . . .

GC: And they could have passed it on to another friend and passed it on and on to all the other animals.

T: But if that is so, a person must have had an idea before they had the word for the idea. So that thought must have come first.

GC: [playfully] Yeah! 'What shall I call it?'

T: Does anyone want to say anything else? Yes?

C: Who taught God?

Many teachers will hear the ring of reality about this exchange, with its divergence and the irrelevance of God to the direct invention of language. But with a class so young it is very interesting to see the girl, GC, introduce an idea quite at odds with the prevailing view. She subsequently managed to persuade over half the class that language not only could, but must have, come first. I hope it doesn't seem far-fetched to say that her statement contains exactly the following ideas, which I express in adult intellectual language:

Despite the theological-provision argument, I think that language is a human construction or invention; furthermore it is based on a semantic relationship, and the semantic is entirely arbitrary. Finally, the invention becomes a cultural or inter-generational possession which we transmit also to non-human animals.

Wider reflections

I have made clear that I regard the learning in this lesson as logically powerful. I should defend that claim. The three-year-old who says 'All gone', and immediately, on seeing another, says 'Some there' is revealing a grasp of the concepts of universal claim and counter instance. She would be utterly confused by someone who seemed to make both claims simultaneously, because she has an appropriate sense (I might call it an 'intuition') of contradiction. What she exhibits is a profoundly satisfying match of logical/sensory understanding; it is exactly suited to the demands made on it by a three-year-old.

What worries me is that the age-related increased demands made on this understanding are not at all addressed by schooling, and that the ensuing failure of education renders school-leavers (and indeed many of my post-graduate students) unable to stand up for themselves intelligently, and renders them fodder for the tabloid culture. They are failing not because of some innate lack of intelligence, but because their logical intelligence has been deliberately untouched by their schooling. They have not learned to listen with appropriate logical scorn to media experts who start: 'Everybody thinks that we should all be . . .' If our school-leavers were to be educated to know what a universal claim is, of the extreme difficulty in establishing one and that a single counter instance knocks one to extinction, I suspect we would hear less of them every morning on political interviews.

With regard to the lesson, there are so many directions in which it could go, depending on the interests of the teacher and the curriculum demands. Most teachers and all children are interested in the imagination, so that could now be the focus of attention. I twice tried it: 'Once upon a time there was a universe in which there was no such thing as imagination, and in that universe a man . . .' This was as volatile as anything I had tried, though I should say it came after the earlier learning to be open and to understand the wide and liberating conventions of the approach. The strategy is as appropriate to specifically approaching any curriculum concepts as it is to exploring contradiction as a feature of thinking. It is a means of interrogating, investigating and validating concepts. In science I have used it to explore the animal/human contrast; in the arts, the art/craft distinction. No teacher who listens is short of ideas that children need to and wish to explore.

Some teachers and academics who have heard my claims have said that these children are dealing with very esoteric matters that most children would be turned off by. When they see my video and transcript evidence, they change their minds. I should draw attention to the mundaneness of the material to which they refer. What I value about this is that it is the children who are bringing forward examples that support or reject a case. I value the ordinariness of the 'grass', FA Cup, television, landscapes, etc, which they, not I, have introduced to the conversation. However, I am also delighted when they do introduce words that I have brought in. So much of schooling has no tincture of the children's common sense about it. It is thereby inert or sterile, and has only the advantage that it is soon forgotten. There is a degree of paradox about my claim that, though I urge the introduction of novel thought strategies and ideas, it is vital to the success of my endeavour that they be richly embedded in the existing syntax and semantics of children's minds. The pragmatics is new. We shall examine these issues in greater detail when we have a greater familiarity with the range of classroom practice.

An example of a novel thought strategy and idea, one I have never heard mentioned as appropriate to children of our age concern, is meta-thinking. I think that it is vital that both children and teachers explore children's meta-thinking, as a means of improving their thinking. The following exchange is only valuable if the children are as familiar with the 'strange' word as they are with the familiar. They prove that they are, by the most demanding of criteria, the ability to chart new territory with it and to resist the teacher's denunciation!

The word 'meta-thinking' is well established in our active vocabulary. We come finally to talk about language about language and I ask if there is a word for that idea. Of course they hit upon 'meta-language', a suggestion I pour scourn on. Note that under my provocation, Jody's immediate statement of resistance is faltering, but recognisably coherent and strong, especially in the light of Amy's formulation. Amy has had the benefit of Jody's efforts:

VQ: Yes, but why would it be that word?

J: It is because I said that 'meta' is before 'thinking', when . . . that's . . .? We call it meta-thinking because you're thinking about thinking. So if we take 'thinking' away and I was talking about 'language', and I was speaking language, so put 'language' there instead of 'thinking', after 'meta'.

VQ: What a stupid suggestion! Isn't that stupid, Amy?

A: No it isn't stupid, Mr Quinn.

VQ: Why do you think it's a good suggestion, Amy?

A: I think it is good because 'meta' is like meta-thinking, is like thinking of thinking and if you were thinking of language you could just take 'thinking' away and put 'meta' there instead of 'thinking' and you would have 'meta-language'.

VQ: You are dead right. You are dead right. Well done. Anyhow, that shows you are still thinking after a whole hour of thinking. A whole hour's meta-thinking. OK. Out you go.

I believe that the children are showing the same vigour of thought here that they would about other things of which they were sure. But it is upon intelligence that they are relying, not recollection, not the authority of the text book and certainly not upon the authority of the teacher. It is the hallmark of good critical thinking teaching, that children are possessed of the credentials, the sources and the intelligence with which to interrogate the subject matter however commonplace, however dependent upon an authority for its introduction, or (as here) however removed from the previous commonplaces of the learners' human experience.

Chapter 3

What is the world?

This lesson has succeeded many times with reception and young infants. I present it here with Year 1 in mind, with occasional references to the sorts of differences I would make further up the primary school. A modicum of acting ability helps get the children wanting to help, and entering the spirit of the enquiry.

Lesson plan

Aims

I want the children to

- express their mis/understanding of the world and space
- explore these understandings, prompted by peers and me
- identify scientific misconceptions needing development
- develop compassion and frankness about fear, especially of ridicule about incomprehension
- develop intellectual courage.

Introduction

On the carpet, I tell the children: 'My friend Samantha, who is your age, told me a secret about something she was ashamed of. She said they had studied the world and space in her class, but that she didn't really understand it. Some kids found out and were nasty to her, and she is afraid to tell the teacher in case she gets laughed at. I told Samantha that I was teaching you and you understood it, so what I could do is ask you the questions, and tell her the answers you give. This would be good because there are some things I don't really understand about space, so I might learn too. I asked her about keeping the secret and she said that she would really like it if I did that. Now, do you mind helping me to help Samantha?' If I've played my cards right, all the earnest little faces nod vigorous assent.

Development

I start with 'a really difficult question': 'WHAT IS THE WORLD?' (said slowly and seriously). I ask for no answers yet, no hands up, just thinking about it, to get a good simple answer.

I have never failed to get 'It's a ball' as one of my first three answers. I say that Samantha can't understand then why you couldn't play football with it. 'Size' is the regular first response, and already the potential questions are cascading:

- How do people know it's a ball, if everybody lives on it?
- How big is it, and how did we find out?
- Well, could giants play football with it?
- If you could shrink it by magic, it wouldn't be a problem, would it? [I sometimes do magic with classes, and claim I could shrink it, and then play with it.]

The diversity of their objections is a delight. Obvious points are:

- the earth's hardness – sore toe
- wet your feet in the ocean
- smash the houses and people
- jolt the world and the people would fall off/down.

Inevitably there will be an opening for an altogether deeper exploration of the world and space. I look for comments such as:

- What would you have to stand on, to play?
- If you tried to head the ball, you couldn't force yourself.
- If you kicked the ball it would just go up and up and up.
- You would have no friends to play. [Some say this because you shrunk the world; some because they would all be too small.]

At every point until near the end, I find difficulties with their accounts, making my questions somehow plausible by reference to Samantha's need to understand, or my need to deal with her problems. It is easier if

I can be the demon myself, and those possessed of drama skills can do this by donning a hat, or otherwise establishing a convention.

Conclusion

I end with a drawing together, now supportively and appreciatively, of the various helpful points that have come forward, and with remaining questions. Reference to Samantha is important.

Analysis

The nurture of attitude is as important as anything in this lesson. My strategy works well for me in developing the attitude of wanting to help. This is so important as it has to do with the spirit of co-operation, so often missing. The anonymity of Samantha is a help, since it allows the children to imagine her helplessness. They are prompted to take her vicariously under their wings, and to forget what spite, former enmity or whatever they might have for a real person. They enjoy her letting them in on her secret. The fund of goodwill that even the playground bully is capable of is a reassuring thing, when little else is. Even the less able are aroused when their superiority of understanding is called upon. The skill is in sustaining this feeling into the critical thinking, and through it to the end when all feel that they have given their bit to the concluding remarks which deserve such praise.

Clearly the lesson as I describe it is designed for exploration rather than transmission. But there are times when there are points you just cannot forbear to correct. I shall mention a few. The direction of the exploration is in your control, reflecting both your own turn of mind and your current curriculum concern. I shall illustrate the exploration by reference to my own turn of mind, hoping that you can easily transfer the points to yours.

Undoubtedly there is a problem of differentiation with this material. Children, fortunately, do not come to school with blank-sheet minds about space, many having seen space pictures, simulations, useful fiction etc. The fact that it is the children who raise the complex problems, that they disagree, that you slow things down by repeating, etc, does sustain the general level of attention. It is trite to say that it does so, far better than I could do if I were transmitting. But if this is a twenty-minute lesson, I will almost always have one or two interludes when they form buzz-groups, when I ensure that the silent ones prepare something to say. These buzz-groups are some of the hardest in all of schooling. Some children easily get bored by not having the attention of the teacher and the whole class for their wisdom. Their hands are up after twenty seconds and they have lost sight of the fact that the group has been told that they are to help each other to think. Real education isn't easy. Immediately after the breaks, the focus for me is not on resuming a good exchange, but on ensuring that the reticent ones have their say, with whatever prompting it takes.

Three ideas of children intrigue me on this topic: where you would play with the world, the world in relation to space, and physical forces in space. I was astonished and delighted on the first occasion that I tried the lesson when I was unsuspectingly but confidently led into this first topic. Piaget, I suspect, had prejudiced me into the negative expectation that they would not be capable of the mental operation of noticing that with the shrunken ball I would need something other than the world to play on. I don't recall how I came out of that exchange. I think I was too excited to think. When it came up again, I used the argument that I would get one of those huge American diggers, and dig out a whole football field, before I shrunk the world. Some objections to this were that the ball would fall over the edge; the more satisfying ones had to do with where I would rest the digger, or where I would deposit the field. The fact that the problem is fanciful or silly does nothing to diminish the value of children's developing the resources to solve it. Their solutions are drawing, as I shall argue, on their own wits and common sense. Their answers are not drawing on the physics they have learned, as they would do later.

So it is with the second of my directions of fascination. The world in relation to space comes up in a range of ways. When the children think of the world in space, they often think of it as having no gravity. So if I could head the ball, I would not be pulled to it, and it would float off indefinitely from me. Its new size might be a consideration, of course, and it would also be the consideration which requires me, in the view of many children, to wear a space-suit; there must in their view be no atmosphere around this new plaything world.

A second question about the world in relation to space came up a number of times. Is the world in space, or is space way out there away from the world? I had not thought before that we, adults and children, work perfectly happily with two quite different concepts of 'space' (and others) without getting confused. But children will argue quite strongly about which meaning is right, often unable to see that this is a conceptual, not an empirical issue. Similar critical thinking is needed across the curriculum: they must learn that a square can have two sides – a left and a right – and also four sides. Again they must see this as a conceptual matter, a matter about identical naming of two different things.

Children reveal their grasp of physical forces in space through this lesson. Momentum and thrust are reasonably well understood. I suspect that cartoons are rich sources of learning here, and even the impossible delays in cartoons, far from wrong-footing children, nudge them to reflect on the impending movement. Older children, as I said earlier, bring school-based misunderstandings of physics into play, and it is most useful to have these identified. One 'astronaut-footballer' of my recollection had the window of his space-ship broken by the ball, which 'let all his gravity out, so he was weightless, and the gravity dragged him out the window'.

With a reception class I once asked (with a misleading question), 'If the world is a ball and I drive a big nail into it, I would puncture it. Wouldn't I?' 'No', I was told. 'There isn't air in it. Just rocks and stuff.' 'There is air,' said another. 'There's creatures in it that need air to live. My dad says worms do.' 'Anyhow the world isn't a ball,' protested a third. 'It's a sophia.'

I don't think that I make inordinate claims for this work when I say that it is some of the most important intellectual experience children can have. They are systematically freed from the regular right-answer, 'supposed-to-be' orientation. They are forced to rely on what understandings they have, with school learning coming in if they can show its relevance. They have a sense of audience or even social purpose for their deliberations, for someone's feelings and self-image are at stake. They are revealing and engaging, in Vygotsky's phrase, their different Zones of Proximal Development, and they are showing the teacher much about where they need, and are ready, to go.

Chapter 4

Tales and the shoplifting tale

This chapter uses a story from published material, free to all schools. It represents both the rest of the high-quality lesson plans in the material, and the increasing use of stories to get children thinking. I will detail a range of such sources, so that the value of this lesson, if it works for you, can be extended very far. The published material is *You, Me, Us!* and is available in response to requests on school paper, from The Citizenship Foundation (CF) at PO Box 999, Sudbury, Suffolk CO10 6FS. I quote the story and some teacher's guidance on its treatment, with permission of the Foundation, which is performing a huge service to high-quality, reflective moral education.

Stories are a wonderful source of thinking. Unlike text books, stories are written to catch and retain attention through a mix of narrative flow, the interplay of character, the identification with certain characters, the involvement in issues, etc. If they are given the chance, children need little pushing to raise a wide range of points about any story. The story almost uniquely gives them the resources to develop issues of motivation, of meaning, of hypotheticals, of parallels with their lives, of possibility etc, and, as in this story, of value. The story has the edge on real life, in that the children are distanced from accusations of wrong-doing; the vicarious distance permits the crucial decentring.

The story: a problem for Mr and Mrs Shah

Mr Shah could not sleep. He was worried. His wife said he was always worrying about something. This was true but this time Mr Shah thought it was serious.

The trouble was that their shop was on the corner of Downham Road, right next to Downham Road Primary School, and every day children came in to buy sweets, crisps, drinks and toys to take to school. Then, in the summer, they came in again on the way home for ice creams and more drinks.

'Where they get the money from, I don't know,' he used to say to his wife, shaking his head. But Mr Shah was a good shopkeeper and he had a knack of knowing just what his children would like, so that year by year the amount the children spent went up and up.

At the wholesalers, he would stand and look at a new range of sweets and say: 'Yes, my children will like those.' He always called them 'his children'. And to this day he has never made a wrong choice.

So why was Mr Shah so worried? His worry had been growing for a long time. He had a problem in the shop and he did not know what to do about it. As he lay awake in bed, it went over and over in his head. He tossed and turned and eventually woke his wife.

'What's the matter, dear?' she said.

'It's my children,' he said.

'They're not your children,' said Mrs Shah. 'Let their parents worry about them. Go back to sleep.'

'It's not as simple as that. Some of the children are stealing from the shop.' Suddenly Mrs Shah was awake.

'What?' she said, sitting up and switching on the light. 'How do you know?'

'I see them, that's how I know,' Mr Shah said. 'I watch them doing it.'

'All of them?' said his wife. 'You watch them?'

'It's not all of them, of course. Most of the children are perfectly honest. It's just a few.'

'Well then, if you know who it is, you can tell the police, can't you?' Mrs Shah protested.

'That's just it,' Mr Shah replied, his voice rising, 'I don't want to involve the police. I don't want to get these children into that kind of trouble.'

'But if they're stealing from us, they deserve to get into trouble. I'm going to call the police myself, right now.'

'Calm down, my dear, it's four o'clock in the morning. The police won't thank you if you call them now. Besides, it's not such a lot of money.'

'But it is to us,' insisted Mrs Shah. 'This is how we earn our living. How would they like it if people were stealing from their parents? That is money stolen from their family.'

'One or two of them don't have any money,' said Mr Shah thoughtfully. 'I know young Jimmy Spencer gets no breakfast in the morning.'

'But that still doesn't make it right to steal,' Mrs Shah insisted. 'I would rather give him a packet of crisps than have him steal them. He is going to get into bad habits.'

Mr Shah was quiet for a moment. 'I suppose we could stop selling the stuff the children come in for,' he said. 'At least then I wouldn't have to worry about the problem.'

'And would you be happy then?' said his wife, looking at her husband's troubled face. He looked at her. She knew what the answer would be.

'I'd hate it,' he said.

As a lesson, I treat this story in two ways. My wife, Trisha, used the story to analyse its potential, as part of an MEd dissertation. She used it in two ways. First, she read the story twice to her Year 5 class, and got them to answer a questionnaire on it. Second, she invited me to take the full class and then a group of five, to explore the moral education potential of the story. Her transcript and questionnaire provide me with a most useful source to freeze and capture dynamic moments, many of which happen too fleetingly in classrooms for us to realise their significance for advancing critical thinking. I also use her excellent analysis of these sources, to draw your attention to general features of the teaching.

Lesson plan

Aims

- explore moral issues to do with stealing
- examine moral and imaginative responses to a story
- look at reasons other than 'getting into trouble' for avoiding wrong-doing
- explore feelings of wrong-doing
- develop the idea of conscience
- consider the place of others.

Introduction

I have used the story without introduction. It 'tells' well, despite a lack of colour, illustration etc. However, having read it you may think it wise to prepare them for a story that will make them think. I would generally think it unwise to introduce it as a story for moral education. The expectation of many children is that moral stories are fables, in which virtue wins and evil suffers. That is quite the opposite of the spirit in which both CF and I put the story forward. However, your knowledge of your class is the sure guide to introducing it.

The following section details CF's thinking in introducing this story:

A problem for Mr and Mrs Shah

Key ideas

- shoplifting as a crime
- victims of crime
- consequences of crime
- punishment

This story is about shoplifting and its consequences both for the shopkeeper and the people involved. Mr Shah runs a corner store near a school and becomes aware that some of the children are regularly stealing sweets from him. His 'problem' is what to do about the problem. On the one hand, he would like the children to stop stealing. He has no wish to see them develop bad habits and besides, he is losing money regularly because of the thefts. On the other hand, he realises that children often do not think clearly about their actions and is fairly understanding, at least to the point of not wishing to get the children into serious trouble.

Stealing from shops is one of the commonest forms of crime involving children and young people. For whatever reason they do it, they often have too little regard for the consequences of their actions and this story is really designed to help them understand that on the receiving end even of minor shoplifting offences are real people who feel the effects.

Below are some of the issues you could explore arising from this story.

Remember to ask the children if they would like to raise any issues of their own for discussion.

Moral reasoning

- Why is Mr Shah worried? Is he right to be worried, in your opinion?

- Do you agreee with Mrs Shah that shoplifting in a small way can lead to bad habits? What does this mean and how might it happen?

- Most people agree that shoplifting is wrong but they might give different reasons for believing this. Work in pairs or small groups to think of as many reasons as you can why shoplifting is wrong. Share your ideas with the class and see how many reasons you can come up with in all. Pick out what you think are the best reasons as to why shoplifting is wrong. Which reason does the class as a whole think is the best reason?

- Think of all the choices open to Mr Shah. What do you think would be the best thing for him to do?

- What would be the best thing that could happen to the children, in your opinion?

- Mr Shah is not keen to see the children punished. Mrs Shah believes they should be punished. Who do you agree with and why?

- Mr Shah has always been kind and friendly to all the children in the shop. Why do you think some of them are stealing from him? Are they being unkind or ungrateful to Mr Shah personally?

- Would it be fair if Mr Shah stopped selling sweets altogether? Who would it be unfair to? Can you think of other examples where crime (e.g. stealing cars) unfairly causes problems for innocent people?

- Does the local school have any kind of duty to do anything in this situation, in your opinion? Why? What can schools do in situations like this?

- What arguments might you use to persuade the boys in this story that what they were doing was wrong? Write them down and compare your arguments with those of others. Which do you think they might listen to?

Thinking things through

- There is an old saying, 'Spare the rod and spoil the child.' What do you think this means and how much do you agree with it? Have a class debate on discipline – is it necessary and what is the best kind of discipline?

- Thinking about wrong-doing in general, draw up a list of things we should take into account when considering whether an action is wrong. In other words, how do we know if something is wrong? Make a list of the things we might look for.

- Do you think that children who 'get away with' one kind of crime are more likely to commit other kinds of crime? Why do you think this?

- Why do you think stealing is so common? How serious a problem is it generally, in your opinion?

- If Jimmy Spicer claimed that he was stealing from the shop because he was hungry in the morning, would that be a reason or an excuse for his action? What do you think is the difference between a reason and an excuse?

Here is a list of statements: are they *reasons* or *excuses*?

'I'm sorry I'm late, Miss, I couldn't find my homework.'

'I'm sorry I'm late, Miss, I've been to the dentist.'

'I admit I stole the pen from the shop. I didn't have anything to write with.'

'I admit I stole the pen from the shop. My friend told me to do it.'

'Yes, I was speeding, officer, my wife is having a baby and I have to get her to the hospital urgently.'

'Yes, I was speeding, officer, I was late for work.'

Try making up some of your own.

Community building

- Have you or your family ever been affected by theft? Share your experiences. How do you think it feels to be the innocent victim of a crime?

- Find out how much of a problem stealing is to the school as a whole. In what way is the life of the school affected by stealing?

- How do you think people in your local community are affected by stealing? Is it a lot or a little? You could invite a local police officer to talk to you about the extent of stealing in your area. In what ways are people affected by it?

Organisation

There is a big advantage in having the children in circle, if this can be arranged, for the full-class discussion. A photocopy of the story is needed for the detailed work of analysis. Flexibility is needed for working in groups and for a return to plenary presentation.

Development (One)

The story is read, either by me or by the children taking a sentence in turn. The latter way is recommended by Matthew Lipman who pioneered this use of stories with children. If each child has a copy, it has advantages other than those of encouraging reading, but it does slow the pace of the lesson, and can diminish the impact of the story. There is a case for reading the story twice. The children sense from this that there is something special to be looked for in it, and they do get a deeper idea of it. This relaxed approach may be against many forces in school and may be a luxury that cannot be afforded. But there are so many things done superficially in many schools, so that their real potential is not felt and it would be better if they were not done.

The standard way in which I have taken the story is to give some time (three minutes) to silent consideration of questions or comments that each child would like to put. These can then be written on a flip-chart, OHP or board and the children can decide which one they would like to discuss. The CF materials and Lipman emphasise the value of this democratic process. I have taught the lesson both ways.

With the topic decided, I usually spend time with the full class allowing them to draw attention to the richness of the topic, the issues it raises and some of the complexity of the issues, at their level. A degree of disagreement is most useful, especially if the children are not used to a teacher celebrating disagreement, rather than 'resolving' it. Depending on the time available, I like to allow a time when the children can work in small groups, with the brief that they discuss, for report back, one or more of the issues that has come out of the chosen topic. This leads to the report back, with or without an opportunity for questioning.

The report back can be the conclusion, or the teacher can highlight a number of issues, disagreements, changes of mind or clarifications that have come about in the course of the lesson. I strongly prefer to end thus, since many children have to learn that in discussion lessons like this (not just moral ones) there is a different set of aims or desired outcomes from those of a more instructional or mechanical skill- or information-acquisition lesson. The force of my preference will be clear when, in the second 'Questions' chapter, I indicate children's expectations about the place of open questions.

Development (Two)

The second development is to give the children a questionnaire imme-diately before the story. Trisha did it thus, and her lesson plan was simply to issue the questionnaire (Figure 4.1), check that the formal details on it were completed, read the story twice and have them com-plete the questionnaire in private silence, giving help in writing to those (two) who would struggle. When Trisha did teach it thus, she proceed-ed the next day to have a lesson as described under Development One. For that reason, I shall say just a little here analysing Development Two specifically, and then treat both approaches together.

Analysis of Occasion One: the questionnaire
The questionnaire approach has one huge advantage. It allows you to have access to more individual responses than if you immediately go

Name _____ Year _____ Age _____ Y _____ M Date _____

YOU ARE ASKED A NUMBER OF QUESTIONS ABOUT THE STORY. AFTER EACH ANSWER, WRITE 'WHY' ON A NEW LINE AND GIVE YOUR REASON.

1 What is interesting to you about the story? Why?

2 What question would you like to ask about it? Why?

3 What would you do if you saw someone shoplifting? Why?

4 Do you feel sorry for anyone in the story? Why?

5 Is it wrong to steal? Why?

6 Is there any situation a person could be in where they should steal? Give your reason.

7 What do you like about the story? Why?

8 What do you not like about it? Why?

9 Is the story finished? Why do you say that?

10 How should it end? Why?

Figure 4.1 Questionnaire (The Citizenship Foundation)

into full-class discussion. For example, there is no surprise that Question 5 ('Is it wrong to steal?') gained universal assent. But the following Question 6 ('Is there any situation a person could be in where they should steal?') gained six affirmatives. I am convinced that private work is preferable here to responses that come after the class members have indicated their views. With the latter, the dangers of undue influence are very great.

I think that the wording of Question 1 ('What is interesting to you about the story?') was of great importance. The little words 'to you' make, for many children, all the difference between a confusing search for a mysterious objectivity, and the real point of the question. However often we tell children about the lack of right answers, we need to do more than tell some of them. We need to word our questions so as to reinforce the point. Question 2 ('What question would you like to ask about it?') reaffirms that a subjective response is sought.

By the time the children get to Questions 5, 6, 9 and 10, about the wrongness of stealing, whether the story is finished and how it might end, they are not in doubt that their views are being sought, even though they may well hold those views as absolutes.

At the same time as this softening of objective edges is taking place, the children are regularly confronting the follow-on question: 'Why?' There is no celebration of subjectivity, as the demands of reason are constantly made. In fact, it might be considered that this questionnaire is too exacting for eight-year-olds, with so many 'Whys?' I do not think so. Children can and must learn that between hard objectivity and 'anything goes' subjectivity, there is a crucial band of intersubjectivity, that is driven through with standards. This band, as much in morality as in science, art evaluation or history, has to do with standards of reasonableness.

From this point, the text is taken from Trisha's dissertation and is in her voice, both about her questionnaire lesson and about my interactive lesson. I have altered the quotations in minor ways to remove material relevant to her technical concerns to do with Kohlberg, Piaget etc. Trisha writes:

The responses to the questionnaire generally confirmed the appropriateness both of the story and the questionnaire in eliciting 'real' moral views from the children. I scare-quote the word 'real' because I want to demarcate it from other, potential meanings. I do not mean 'autonomous' and certainly do not mean 'authentic'. The meaning is the actual views that children profess at this age. Many of the ideas expressed may be derivative, unconsidered, even contradictory.

Question 6 is an interesting case. Coming after the question 'Is it wrong to steal?', it asks: 'Is there any situation a person could be in where they should steal?' Six children responded affirmatively, giving as reasons homelessness and starvation. This is not necessarily contradictory of their answer that it is wrong to steal; they might interpret the earlier question as an 'in general' question, rather than a 'universal'. But a more mature response would deal with the discrepancy in the two answers.

The earlier responses to Question 5 ('Is it wrong to steal? Why?') show the unsurprising range that the research literature would lead one to expect. The common phrases are

- not very nice
- it's against the law
- you code get in to sereo's truddell by the polise
- chos you are going to get cort
- this is a saying don't do to people what you don't like to be done to you
- you could be sent to jail
- cause we have to pay four the stuff for you to buy
- Mr Shah has got to pay for the things that they steal
- because stealing doasn't get you eney were
- you will have to pay for the things you steal
- your mother and father will be cross

Through the children's writing here one can hear the voice of the elders, variously interpreted and experienced, when not quite parroted. But there may be other voices, such as 'the over people will be upset'. It is not possible without probing to say whether this is genuine altruism, or parroting.

Despite the divergence and greater authenticity in these responses (to an admittedly psychological rather than moral question), there is a very interesting homing tendency on the second most interesting thing, Mr Shah's motives:

Why didn't he . . .

- phone the police?
- shout at the children?
- stop worrying?

and he

- is so carme
- gets all upset cause he dous'end wo'nt to get the children into trubell by the police
  etc.

But undoubtedly the predominant interest is in the morality of the tale. This could be a reflection of this question coming first, and their having the sense of duty to mention this. Reworking the questionnaire would test this conjecture, and it would be interesting to do so, because of course it was the avoidance of such leading that I was striving for.

The conceptual, empathic, emotional and literacy diversity that I sought can be illustrated over and over again. In response to Question 4 ('Do you feel sorry for anyone in the story? Why?'), Mr Shah was by far the favourite object. The couple come next, followed by the breakfast-less Jimmy Spicer. But there were delightful meta-narrative responses, like the rest quite unprompted, such as:

No not Relly. Why? Case it is dust a story.

and

I donet fiel sorry for eney whon. becoues no boddys dun enething for me to fiel sorry for

This last quotation, in its confidence, evinces not just a freedom in interpreting literature, but also a freedom from empathic expectation. It too is a meta-reflection, in that it is questioning the assumption in the question, that there is an object of pity or empathy. I see this without reservation as a good thing, in that it reveals an intelligence not bound by adult expectation. In this case such a judgement is easier to assert than it would be if the child were dealing with a right-answer question. And even there I would defend the error-making freedom.

An opposite view can be seen in the case of a child who is too engrossed in the story's content. She has difficulty in distinguishing her feelings about the story from her feelings about the topic. In response to Question 7 ('What do you like about the story? Why?') she writes:

I hate shoplifting storeis. because it is not nice

At the same time it is interesting to note that this pupil, perhaps because of her extreme revulsion from shoplifting stories, responds unusually to Question 10 ('How should it end? Why?'). The others go for a plot to end it; she goes for a theme:

> I think it should end were the children stopped shoplifting.

Many responses to Question 3 ('What would you do if you saw someone shoplifting? Why?') were very punitive. Almost everyone would call the police, and most would inform the shopkeeper or manager. There was no evidence here of the concepts of mitigation, of first offence etc, but the instrument clearly did allow for these to be raised, if only by the strength of the children's reactions. Again there was evidence of divergence in one case, who probably knew he was expressing a 'wrong' view in writing:

> I would see who it is and if it is my mate I wouln'nt tell but I would worn him. Why? Because I'm a mate to him and I dont tell on on my mates.

I was fascinated by the fact that there was not the divergence of response to the morality of the narrative that there was to the other, 'psychological' (e.g. interest) features. I shall speculate now as to why this is the case, and on the significance of this for my central purpose.

Questions 5 and 6 are the ones which most directly address morality ('Is it wrong to steal? Why?' and 'Is there any situation a person could be in where they should steal? Give your reason'). In these there was not just agreement on the morality of theft, but considerable agreement in the reasons given. (I have already dealt with the major exception, the occasional, circumstantial justification of stealing.) I believe that the major reason for this is that moral ideas have already been transmitted to the children, along with reasons, and they are expecting to have these called upon when an appropriately worded question is presented. It is not just the precept that has been successfully transmitted; the experience of 'getting into trouble' is very real for those who have been found transgressing. Some of the reasons given strike me as transmitted rather than discovered. For example, in response to Question 5 ('Is it wrong to steal? Why?'), 'Yes because stealing doasn't get you eney were' seems an implausible, empirical, universal claim. It is a happy ending feature of the fiction children watch and read, as it is a 'moral' injunction often expressed, but it is unlikely to be based on their lived experience. Whatever should happen, many of them will know that with a modicum of skill, the profits of stealing are substantial.

One interesting feature of divergence on the moral questions is the development of tautologous answers. In particular, the simpler questions, such as 'Is it wrong to steal? Why?' had what I think of as more advanced answers which drew attention to the undesirable consequences of stealing, e.g. 'Somebody always ends up in trouble'. Another child drew attention to three relevant features, 'alot of trouble', paying for the things, and mother's and father's anger. On the other hand there are answers like 'Because taking something that does not belong to you is wrong'. This is largely tautological, except for the replacement of 'stealing' by a definition of it. This aspect of children's responses had not occurred to me before. I think that it deserves attention, because it reflects a discomfort with the questioning that is not evident in the other answers. I suspect that it has to do with the fact that the answers being given are adult-derivative, and heartfelt, but they are lacking in authenticity. I would like to test this conjecture by comparing responses from children whose moral views were known to me and where those views were on issues that deeply and authentically touch certain children, e.g. the rights of animals.

Analysis of Occasion Two: Quinn's teaching
My brief to Quinn: I asked Quinn to work towards the children seeing the connection between the vicarious condemnation of shoplifting, and their own lives. I asked him to do this largely through questioning, and for the questioning to be exploratory of concepts bearing on morality, and that the questioning would be testing or pushing the boundaries of moral stages, thus operating in the moral Zone of Proximal Development. I also wanted the Shah story brought in incidentally, to see if there was a continuity between the various levels of exploration. Finally, I asked him to concern the children with the process of thinking, so that their learning would have a greater chance of generic advance.

This was a brief that would allow me the freedom not only to watch and analyse the children (albeit largely on video), at a useful, decentring distance from myself, but also to avail myself of Quinn's strength in giving children access to the excitement of ideas. He was happy with the brief, and decided to pursue it in this way:

1 explore the 'getting into trouble' consequence of wrong-doing, so as to set it aside

2 discuss personal examples of theft
3 draw from these examples ideas of the feelings associated with wrong-doing
4 approach the concept of 'conscience' and introduce the word 'conscience'
5 emphasise meta-questioning as the 'process of thinking' feature.

The teaching by Quinn was of considerable interest, both in general, and in relation to seeing the children excited by the idea of developing their moral thinking. I would like to attend to six aspects of his work:

- moving beyond 'getting into trouble'
- the feeling dimension of stealing
- questioning technique to avoid right-answer responses
- the word 'conscience'
- the difference between the feelings of and for Mr and Mrs Shah
- the prevalence of meta-thinking.

Quinn made great efforts early on to get the children to think about what he did not want to develop, the idea of getting into trouble. Many authors alert us to the difficulty of persuading children at this age/stage to think of reasons other than those of getting into trouble, as to why they should be constrained morally. His strategy was to emphasise this set of reasons in order to contrast it with the more internal reasons. On the first page of the transcript the children offer him ten respects in which a child could get into trouble. But he experienced difficulty in securing a sense of irrelevance for the idea. They regularly reverted to it.

He approached this problem in various ways. One way was to put it in general terms: 'Imagine that you do not get into trouble . . .', but this soon reduced to getting into trouble. He tried a more anecdotal approach: '. . . you saw an old lady dropping a wallet and you picked up the wallet. Nobody saw you. You throw the wallet away and keep the money. Nobody would catch you, right, what would you feel about that?' Very soon, having explored the feelings that sound like those of remorse and guilt, they are back with feelings, yes, but of fear and shame, feelings of the prospect of trouble. Their mums would be suspicious of their new-found wealth and expenditure. 'But you might be adults with a place of your own.'

Closely linked with this was his attempt to get them to identify the feelings they would or did have when they had done something wrong. Three of them recounted incidents of their stealing within the home and the feelings that ensued. Both accounts and articulation of feelings were graphic. The children located the feelings in their upper trunk, and the contrast was developed between this feeling and that of 'butterflies in the stomach' as experienced before a race. One girl, with conspicuous frankness, said, 'To be honest, I'd give it back. I'd feel awful.' She was referring to the money taken from the old lady's wallet.

Another girl makes a most promising move later. Knowing that the 'getting into trouble' set of feelings is not what he is after, she moves, I believe, ahead of the others, with a word which I do not think she draws from a source outside of her, 'guiltiness'. The exchange is:

Q: Let's leave that now. This feeling, is there a word for it? Is there a word for that feeling when you have done something wrong?

ALL: Yes.

Q: And it's not that you're afraid of being caught, but you feel, 'Oh, I shouldn't have done it'.

S: It's called 'guiltiness'.

Q: 'Guiltiness', feelings of guilt. Right. What is it that makes you say that, a feeling of guiltiness?

S: When he takes you to court, and judge says, 'Guilty or not guilty?', and you don't know what will happen.

Q: And then your feeling is . . .?

S: Guiltiness.

Q: But you're bringing it back to getting into trouble and I'm thinking of your not getting into trouble.

Quinn acknowledged that, without further evidence, he probably misinterpreted the reference to 'court' as 'getting into trouble'. I agree, and think this is a substantial move towards the concept 'conscience'.

I do think that there is considerable value in children experiencing such hypothetical situations, as developed from the story. At the distance of speculation and hypothesis, and deriving from the vicarious experience of the CF fiction, some children did and do consider the ethics of situations never yet encountered, and they speculate on the ethics without the prospect of immediate personal gain. Thus real gain or temptation is not a factor in their first encounter with the question. Whatever the carry-over to their behaviour, the advantage of Quinn's approach was that they would have gone through some reflection on the ethical questions at a distance from the old lady. Her plight and suffering would be considerations in their hypothetical deliberations. I mention this as I have discussed with children actions where the suffering of consequent victims (e.g. from vandalised trains or phone boxes) is not at all a consideration in the reason to do or avoid it. Whilst consideration of the plight of victims of crime is not a sufficient condition of deterring crime, it is a necessary condition of thus deterring. It is therefore vital that this necessary step be taken, by this vicarious means.

Quinn has developed a questioning strategy which makes allowance, he claims, for the right-answer syndrome in children. At times he systematically misleads children into suggesting answers that he does not believe, in situations where he thinks it reasonable that they will either disagree with his suggestion, or be able on reflection to disagree. There was an extremely interesting example of this in the lesson when he asked the 'trick' question. After a number of failed attempts to get them to move beyond 'getting into trouble', he asks,

Q: Let's say you stole something, and nobody saw you, and you got away with it. That would be alright; wouldn't it?

The initial, unreflecting answer, picking up on Quinn's paralanguage and inviting the affirmative, is 'Yes', followed by a firm 'No'.

This is dangerous pedagogic territory. It is playing with children's susceptibility to be led, and is a questionable practice, particularly in the moral sphere. Quinn is well aware of this and insists on debriefing if a child does go along with his suggestion. On this occasion the attempt to debrief followed immediately:

Q: You said 'Yes' first of all. Do you know why I think you said 'Yes' to begin with? Because of the way I asked the question. How did I ask the question?

T: Nobody saw you and you got away with it.

Q: And what did I say after that?

T: That it would be alright.

Q: Right. Yes, are you trying to say what I said?

DL: You said that, um, no-one saw you and would it be good to get away with it?

Q: No, no, no. If I had said that, I don't think Toni would have fallen into my trap. I said it differently. I said, 'That would be alright. Wouldn't it?' See the difference in those two questions? One is: 'Do you think it would be alright?'

T: Yes.

Q: That's the way you put it; that's different, because I don't think you would have said, 'Yes'. I said, 'That would be alright. Wouldn't it?' See the difference?

S/DL: Yes, yes.

Q: Could you put your finger on the difference?

S: It's sort of saying, 'That would be OK'.

Q: Right, leading her along. [*S nods*] Saying, 'It would be OK', and then a question put at the end.

Whether or not the intervention is successful, I believe it is worth trying. There is much evidence on the videotape of his at other times attempting to lead children, by his questioning, in a direction that he genuinely does believe in. When I questioned him on this, he acknowledged that it was so, that it is always so, and that it is because it is so that he attempts to make allowance for it. There was an instance of his questioning in this predisposing way, which he acknowledged as just such. He had asked if the guilt feeling was using *words* to tell you things, hoping for the answer 'No'. When he got a straight 'Yes', he asked: 'Was it?' in a way that indicated clearly that the supplied answer would not do.

Quinn's practice here is a useful step in self-safeguarding against the danger to which Piaget alerts us:

> The great danger, especially in matters of morality, is that of making the child say whatever one wants him to say. There is no infallible remedy for this; neither the good faith of the questioner nor the precautionary methods which we have laid stress upon elsewhere are sufficient. The only safeguard lies in the collaboration of other investigators.
>
> (Piaget, J., *The Moral Judgement of the Child*, pp. vii–viii)

Quinn was at pains to move, as I have indicated, beyond the idea of 'trouble', and this took another form. He wanted to explore how effective the word 'conscience' would be either in expressing an idea that they were articulating, or in triggering the idea. It is a difficult idea to isolate in this way since it too is an idea and word that children of this age are beginning to encounter at home and in class. So its presence in either their active or passive vocabulary is not to be taken as an indication of authentic reasoning on the children's part. This was the least successful part of Quinn's intervention. The story, however, is a reasonable one for raising the issue. It might be better if, instead of an exclusively entrepreneurial (and even more so, uxorial!) perspective, there was a story with a conflict of interest among tempted children. A story in which there was dialogue between children deterred from stealing by fear of the consequences, and children deterred by expressed reasons of conscience, would probably be a better vehicle for broaching this conflict.

However, there were advances beyond the notion of getting into trouble, as when Gemma asks

> Well, what could you do if you tore the picture up and you realised? What could you do to sort of like make it up to that person?

Gemma has understood both the feeling of bad conscience and the possibility for atonement/reparation.

One issue that seemed to raise itself and surprised both Quinn and me was the children's separate attitudes to the husband and wife in the story. In an obvious sense, Mr Shah is the darling of the story. His tolerance, concern and fellow-feeling for the children is clearly calculated to win the children round to his perspective. Her petulance and confrontational approach is clearly not so designed. And yet in the conversation the children, led ably by Gemma, strongly came down in favour of her feelings in preference to his. This was undoubtedly prompted by what they thought should happen to the children (i.e. they should be punished).

This led me to question my earlier belief that the story was as open as I had thought it was. I speculated that it might not just be weighted in favour of property, but that it might be predisposingly told so that the Mrs Shah attitudes, despite her superficial unpleasantness, would prevail. Clearly I cannot pronounce on the basis of this evidence, but it is so overwhelming in this case, that I would like to extend the study to see if this unexpected feature might be replicated with other, larger samples.

There was a pervasive feature of Quinn's work which I found astonishing. It was the prevalence of meta-thinking on the children's part, prompted by Quinn's meta-questioning. When I asked him about this feature he stressed its importance for developing generic qualities of thinking, in line with my brief. The analogy he used was the Oxfam charity one between supplying a peasant with a fish, or the skill of fishing. However, he was taken aback when I said that every question he asked, for example on the first two pages of the transcript, was an invitation to meta-thinking, either to think directly about their thinking or about the language they had used. He did not attribute this to the particular story but admitted that, as the discovery was fresh to him, he was not in a position to say.

Since the point applies to all of his work, any quotation would illustrate it. The extended quotations above, on 'guiltiness' and on debriefing from the unfairly leading question, show a sustained, second-order concern to deal with thinking and the effect of language on thinking.

I undertook to give details of a wider range of stories and approaches to stories for teaching thinking. Although any story will do, it is probably more confidence-boosting if you work at first with stories that are accompanied by teachers' notes, which at least offer a ready supply of questions. I mention Matthew Lipman's work first, since it has had a profound effect on schools around the world. The stories are specially written for developing not just critical thinking, but philosophy in children. They are about children thinking philosophical ideas, and are a good base for getting readers to identify and take further the issues raised. It must be said, though, that they are very American, a factor that must be contended with. One of these, *Harry Stottlemeier's Discovery*, has been translated into British English by Roger Sutcliffe. The story is a good one for exploring simple but profound logical relationships with secondary-age children. I expect it would also interest many adults at their own level.

Karin Murris has produced a ring-binder kit, *Teaching Philosophy with Picturebooks*, which illustrates my point that books do not need to be specially written. She has collected some of the most widely available books from the infant classroom and supplied a range of questions for each. The approach is a good leveller in that top junior children soon realise that the questions about these 'baby' books are profound. The less able/literate are not disadvantaged as the narrative is picture-assisted and probably already familiar.

Dr Bob Fisher, who has done so much for critical thinking from his base, The Centre for Thinking Skills in Brunel University, has produced an excellent book of stories, *Stories for Thinking*, as well as one

in an extending series, *Games for Thinking*, each with helpful suggestions for use. Richard Fox of Exeter University has written a wonderful range of stories across the primary curriculum. They are genuinely
thought-provoking and based on an intimate knowledge of the life of a
child's mind. His *Maths Lesson*, for example, moves seamlessly from
day-dreaming to questions of personal identity and infinity. The book
is *Thinking Matters: Stories to Encourage Thinking Skills*.

Chapter 5

A lesson of questions

Lesson plan

Aims

- become comfortable in asking questions
- recognise the value of the activity in intellectual growth
- become familiar with some differences between kinds of questions
- articulate questions important to them individually to consider the place of questioning in their own education
- develop meta-thinking on curiosity.

Introduction

Let the children know that this is going to be a different kind of lesson – one in which we will be exclusively concerned with questions. 'I want you to think of the questions, and what I want you to do is to think of as many different kinds of questions as you can. You don't have to know the answer to them, and I hope there will be many that you won't know the answer to. Take three minutes now to think of questions, and write down a few. After three minutes, you can spend another few minutes talking with someone about your questions, and see if you can decide if they are different kinds of questions.'

After a minute, I help the non-starters by saying that they can ask about something from display or a TV programme or sport. I spend the remaining time ensuring the few stragglers have the assistance they need, and have something written. After the discussion time, I call them to silence, and ask them to ensure that every question ends with a question mark.

(Alternative) introduction

I don't allow the preparation and discussion time, but go straight in. The differences are enormous, and both have advantages.

Development

On the second option the work is led by the confident children, who are not inhibited by the unusual approach. There is quite a lot of follow-the-leaders in the kinds of questions, and soon my task is that of identifying the kind of predominant question, and asking them to come up with different kinds. On the first option, some of this work is already done, so that if I ask for serial presentation, I get diversity of kind from the outset.

Whichever option I take, my major concerns, apart from liberating them into this task, are to develop meta-questioning along the lines of my aims above. So I force them to reflect on and express the kind of questioning that is predominating at one time. I ask them to move beyond this kind, and, if I have had the lengthy introduction, this is easy, because I have already had paradigms of question types. In the back of my mind at this stage is the taxonomy of questions presented in Chapter 6, but I am not trying to teach this taxonomy at this stage. Clearly I want to move with some haste beyond a preoccupation with right-answer questions, and I would be surprised if I didn't introduce the moral category, the conceptual, the hypothetical and other categories of major human interest. But other categories will present themselves and my task is to present the greatest diversity I can.

There are a number of directions in which I may move the lesson. I may want to get them asking about areas of current classwork. I may jog them to diverse topics by saying, 'No-one has asked anything about death, animals, space, flowers, god . . .' I may say, 'Are there any questions beginning with "why"?' I may ask for questions that look for differences between things. I may ask for questions that ask others what their feelings or thoughts are on certain topics.

Conclusion

I allow the conclusion to be determined by the way the lesson has gone. The most appropriate end might be to present a selection of questions, along with indication of their category, on OHP, board or flip-chart. Another end is to select a few questions and have a go at discussing them, seeing the difference in methods appropriate. A third end is to ask each child to frame a question that is very interesting to self. They might be asked what is the most interesting question they have heard today. I would ensure that the children are familiar with the idea of questions about questions, and I see no reason why eight-year-olds upwards should not have the word 'meta-questions' in their active vocabulary.

Analysis

The phrase that I most closely associate with the value of this lesson is 'common sense'. In many classrooms, the NC has in practice driven further obstacles between school learning and children's common sense. By 'common sense' I mean the general culture and understanding of things that children bring in such large measure with them to school. Like a modern Asian language, a passion for horses, idiosyncratic curiosities, these do not cross the school gate. The questions lesson reinforces the value of the child's own thinking. This point becomes clear to the child, not because it is clearly stated at the outset, but by the caring listening that the teacher reveals, and encourages in the other children.

The connection between common sense and humour is strong and diverse. A questioning lesson should at some stage exhibit that popular form of children's humour, the leading question and the joke answer. In one recorded lesson for this book we had:

Why did the dinosaur cross the road?
Because they didn't have chickens in them days!

But some of the questions have a different sort of humour. The eight-year-old in Chapter 2's contradiction lesson, who has grappled with the (theological) origins of language, is prompted to ask, 'Who taught God?' It is clear that he knows that this is funny, but he also has a sense of its profundity, of its seriousness for the theological-origin argument. The interest of upper juniors in this question is akin to that in questions like the possibility of an infinity of numbers, and like what is beyond the limits of space or the universe. There is also humour in a complete shift of question type. I give some examples. After a mundane set to start with, I will call for different types, and get such as:

- How many flowers are there?
- Why don't old people run out of new things to say?
- Do we need libraries?
- Would it be good if there were no teachers?
- Why do we have pets?
- How come some kids have no dads?
- What are all the wars for?
- Would it be fair to give animals just the same rights as us?
- When will people stop getting sick?
- Why do some people bully so much?

It is as well to mention here the necessity of avoiding laughing at a child, either for a question asked or for a wrong answer. Children are so often afraid to ask or answer because of the treatment they have had previously. Whilst we can sometimes get the two kinds of laughing mixed up, it is usually clear when there is a nasty undertone. A questioning lesson is a good opportunity to register absolute intolerance of the act of ridicule, and to require a formal apology from the offender.

There is a frustration about a confinement to questions, especially when the children are liberated and produce such rich ones. But dealing with them is simply delayed, though the richness is such that many have to be neglected. It is for this reason that I invite each child to write one question for me to read and answer, because children know that the purpose of questions is to get answers, and they have been prompted to think of questions as they never have before.

There is much force behind a number of sayings about questions and answers. The de-schoolers used to rail against schooling which gives a series of answers across the curriculum to questions that the children wouldn't dream of asking. There is force too in the saying that education is more about questioning answers than about answering questions. But the force crucially depends on whose questions are being answered. The approach here allows us to find the rich source of questioning that is going on in the minds of the children, so that we can attempt a match between that and our curriculum constraints. I like Jacob Bronowski's way, in *The Ascent of Man*:

> It is important that children bring a certain ragamuffin barefoot irreverence to their studies; they are not here to worship what is known, but to question it.

I would use the expression 'what is believed or understood', instead of 'what is known', and I believe that this stifling reverence is more easily prevented if we start, not by questioning *it*, but by questioning.

Any teacher who shares my enthusiasm for this approach will probably have plenty of ideas as to how to follow up, and I have already intimated how the curriculum would reflect the work. This reflection will be as diverse as classrooms are. However, I give a few pointers. A class whose work celebrates critical thinking will have a great preponderance of questions, children's questions as well as teacher's reworking of them. Topics can be based on them, just as well as they can on nouns. CD-ROM work is ideally based on questions. The sense of audience that is so crucial to real writing is fairly easily achieved if the children have a question written to an expert, in the town hall, the government, the Vatican, the university, etc. The probability of a response, they must learn, that is more than token, will depend on how well worked, how well researched the question already is. So the point about the enhanced sense of audience applies to the energy that is put into the research also.

It may be surprising to say that, unusual as this lesson may be to children, I do not think it should be a one-off. Clearly, there is need for a time to digest or process the richness of the first feast, but it is a stepping stone to greater things. Despite best efforts, and whatever opportunities for 'buzz-groups' we make, some children need time to accommodate to this culture. Even those who best accommodate can show greater skill on a second or later occasion. They have found their intellectual and pedagogic feet. The sort of differentiation I have in mind here is not a standard one of ability in classwork. The novelty of this approach identifies a new set of high flyers: those whose strength is not in informational retention, but in curiosity, whose boredom arises from the mis-match referred to earlier. So the repeated novel lesson is not just like introducing a topic like dinosaurs, an activity like chess or a subject like Egyptology. These innovations will normally catch the attention of a new range of children. The questioning approach, when they find their feet, will identify the naturally curious children and the natural curiosities of all the children.

Display is my final point about follow-up. A strong statement is made about the climate of a school, by the presence or absence of questions, as I shall argue in the process chapter on questions. Questions arising from this lesson can be displayed, to achieve and show off the intellectual interaction that some displays should go for. A wonderful meta-question for children is:

In what ways could these questions be arranged so as to make a reasonable grouping, for us and for outsiders to share our interest in them?

Notice the low- and high-order intellectual demands of the following suggestions:

- ones which have five words
- ones which have the question marks missing
- ones which we have found the answer to
- ones which nobody could know the answer to
- ones which the following people want answered
- ones which ask about what it is right to do
- ones which we have written off for answers to
- hard ones.

In this new subject we sell both the children and the subject short if we do not make manifest the major new demands and achievements that characterise it. The scope for improvement in speaking and listening is infinite. But it is not right, for many reasons, to have both the evidence and the further stimulus concealed on tape in a cupboard. It is right to have it both making converts to this approach, and providing the stimulus to curiosity that is at the heart of all good intellectual education.

Chapter 6

In praise of falsity

It astonishes me how neglected falsity is as an educational tool. Almost its only regular use is by the teacher who has had an error spotted by a child and claims, 'You've spotted the deliberate mistake.' I shall argue in this chapter that from the point of view both of content and of method, a great deal is lost by failing to consider its intentional and structured place.

Consider method. There is a sense of release for children told that they can write sentences that are false. The release is akin to humour, and indeed leads to real humour. Imagine the atmosphere in a class of seven- to eight-year-olds as they write the following sentences for display in a circle entitled UNIVERSAL CLAIM: ALL THESE SENTENCES ARE FALSE (EXCEPT THIS ONE):

> Mr Quinn is a slimeball.
> Mr Quinn eats children.
> Mr Quinn hates Class 9.

Imagine their further delight when the rule changes to 'All but one of these sentences is false and made of five words.' Their play then is with identifying the false statement, especially if they still have permission to write things about Mr Quinn, and especially when the brighter ones lead the others in the discovery or decision that a sentence doesn't have to have both criteria, to satisfy the conditional. Their true sentence can then be a secret. The humour is indeed heightened by writing about the teacher, but a similar release comes with most commonsense topics.

Beyond method, consider content. Consider the disappointment of a child whose offering in 'best' is refused because it lacks a full stop or some other feature of a sentence. So often, we try and fail to get children throughout the primary school to write in sentences, but we plead, mark and condemn in a context where the point of formal sentencing is obscure. The passage makes sense to the child as she writes it and often as she reads it. We don't focus on sentences as units, outside of a continuous prose context. True, my method so far uses motivation to reinforce punctuation only at an instrumental level. But it is a short step to the children writing, 'A story made of three, false sentences, each of less than seven words' (with secret permission to err on one of these criteria, once only). Then the children have a deeper attachment to the idea that being properly punctuated is necessary to show success. They are approaching the intrinsic purpose of punctuation. They know that their own joke has backfired if they make a single unintended mistake in any of the three categories. (I deal elsewhere with the value of peer-scribing. This is one area where the skills associated with it can easily be learned to the benefit of both children, author and scribe, since both are concentrating on language skills which need substantial reinforcement.)

I return to method. There is a sense of conspiracy in a class that is let loose on falsity. (Of course I exclude creative fiction from the category I am dealing with.) This sense of conspiracy is heightened when they discover that their display is for use not just in the classroom but in the corridor where it will be seen by others who will not understand, who have no truck with authorised falsity. Since I almost always use questions in display, there is scope for children's meta-thinking about the best questions to attach, to interest and develop those outsiders who look and are inclined to condemn. But that point takes me back to content.

I give examples in curriculum. I ask a class of six-year-olds who have recently done shapes to tell me about a square. 'It has four sides.' 'Well, with a tiny square, you could get away with just three sides. Couldn't you?' I am told you could not, by a girl who takes me on, with surprising confidence on a first meeting. She tells me it would be a triangle, and draws a tiny triangle with her finger. I draw a square, all but the last line (the left side). She tells me that it hasn't got a side. I point to the right side and say it has. Now she tells me that it has to have two sides. I tell her that she's changing the rules, that she said earlier that squares needed four sides. Weakly (for once), she agrees that they do – a loose end on which I would love to have debriefed, commending her grasp of the ambiguously obscured two concepts. I change tack and draw a square in the air, counting the sides as I go but arriving at the destination on the count of three, rather as a child who has not learned one-to-one co-ordination might. She has my measure and tells me, 'You counted wrong.' The headteacher comes to see what's causing the commotion, and we continue to argue. I go further over the top in asking the girl a question and she beautifully judges the situation, saying, 'Stop shouting.'

My role play in this was useful to me, but I can understand it not appealing to some and being difficult for others. It is not necessary. Some of the same educational value can be striven for by raising the issue hypothetically. The values have to do with defending a position in mathematics, and with deepening one's conceptions of maths concepts. I should add, however, that one former senior colleague, having seen the video of the lesson, told me that it was dangerous in that I was undermining or trying to undermine the school's teaching of conservation of number. The educational value that would not be gained without the role play is one I value highly, that of learning to stand up to undue pressure from someone in authority.

Before I proceed to other subjects, I should qualify my argument in a number of ways. I can well understand a quite different form of criticism: moral objection. This was forcibly put to me by Matthew Lipman on an occasion of my representing at a conference my view that it was good to bring undue pressure to bear on children, in a context where they could learn to resist such pressure. He agreed that such learning was an educational good, but argued that the end does not justify the means. His point is even stronger when we consider the additional point that I put to children defences of moral positions that I consider wrong – the equivalent of moral falsehood. Lipman is quite right. My justification is the importance of the end, both of learning to resist the undue influence and of learning to articulate against my moral 'falsehood' the importance, say, of distinguishing two senses of 'fun' when I have defended vandals as '. . . just having fun, like you have fun at ice skating. You shouldn't be stopped. Why should they?'

But a second qualification is ethically relevant to what I do. Debriefing is almost always important. Of course most of the children can identify what is going on. They see the funny side of a teacher deliberately in the wrong. But there may be those who do not and who remain silent through the fun, taking in we know not what, and left wondering. Just the same is true if we try to teach a class what we take to be truth. Debriefing is an opportunity to clear the air and even to explore why falsity was defended.

I hardly ever find a problem with children's understanding of the role change. On one occasion I did have a problem when we were using falsity to work on the construction of complex sentences. I had begun with the arguable falsehood 'Mr Quinn is the most beautiful person in the world', which the eight-year-olds were contradicting, echoing the sentence structure, even as I added adverbs, subordinate clauses, etc. As the class gleefully struggled with the syntax and the various possible ways of contradicting, one poor girl could take no more. 'You are. You are,' she called out. It is difficult for me to say that her fine fellow-feeling, despite her courage (and error), was a sign of social immaturity. At any rate she was incapable of partaking in the role play, because she did not easily enough see it as make-believe. We must be very careful of this feature of differentiation, along with many other ways in which individuals and groups may not share a common understanding, and may mask this failure.

I have also been criticised within the Society for Advancing Philosophical Enquiry and Reflection in Education (SAPERE) for a failure to establish a contract with children prior to such role play, a common practice in drama lessons. I well appreciate that it is often better to do so, especially if there is a danger that the children will feel duped. I resist the pressure on many occasions, for two reasons. First, the children do comprehensively get the better of me, so that the idea of dupery has not come up when either a class teacher or I have explored the experience. But more importantly, there would be something about the declaration of a contract that would seriously undermine my intention. It is important that they develop the courage to disagree with this adult, not because they have been told to, or told that they may, but because they come to believe that, authority adult that he may be, he is in the wrong.

With these qualifying points out of the way, I proceed to a wider range of curriculum illustration.

I often approach science from the point of magic, which is science's falsehood. I normally do this in role, claiming to be magic, but to make it more accessible, I will describe the lesson in a hypothetical way, with occasional references to the role. I do an irrelevant magic trick and then another. The second is that I say a magician can pour water into a bottle that is upside down. I then place a hot empty milk bottle upside down in a pyrex dish which has coloured, cold water in it. I pour more cold water over the bottle and as I do, the bottle and the air inside cool and contract so that the coloured water is sucked in and up. Is this magic? Is science defeated? It's good to do it again, to watch the intense concentration. If in role, I claim that my magic works once only, and they have great fun as they discover that it is working, the second time. I refuse to look, claiming to know from my education and books 'what happens and what doesn't.' But out of role, there is the important and educationally potent concentration and desire to explain without magic, to explain magic away. First attempts by top juniors often deal with condensation and evaporation. With whatever prompting is needed, there is a breakthrough to heat-loss as the factor. My claim in role is that I heat the bottle to sterilise it. The same claim could be put as part of the magic hypothesis, and part of their successful explanation is dismissing this.

When they discover that heat-loss is the factor, and that the process is reversible, the learning can be taken further by getting them to imagine other hypotheses that they could test to see if it is always so. I am equipped with more bottles, balloons, plastic bottles with tops, and I hope, access to a fridge and freezer compartment. As they speculate about hypotheses, the 'magic' perspective can be put as:

- Do you really think the heated bottle would expand the balloon covering the bottle's mouth?
- And as the bottle is cooled again, it would suck it back in, you think?
- But why would the plastic bottle crumple in the freezer?
- I mean it doesn't lose any air with the top tight on, does it?

There are many values being sought here. The relevant ones are that the children are invited to choose an explanation against an initially implausible one, and then against adult pressure that there is something suspect about their developing alternative. They are forced to rely upon the deep structure of the empirical method, of the sensory and hypothetico-deductive method of explanation, against a teacher's putting worries about their speculation. It is abject failure and my lack of judgement, if they are cowed, if they refuse to persist. But it succeeds as they overcome the negative suggestion and take strength from the empirical vindication and the compounding strength of their sequentially confirmed hypothesis.

The disconfirmation of wrong hypotheses is also important, and this too can be made the object of deep critical learning. As always, the question 'Why?' must be prominent, in this case both to identify the reason the idea was not confirmed, and to explore why it had seemed plausible in the first case. Again judgement is required in deciding which wrong hypotheses can usefully be explored. The earlier one about condensation I would not attempt, in this context, as it involves earlier learning in science and different equipment. Explanation alone without experiential learning would be of little avail.

The heated bottle covered with a balloon leads, however, to another wrong but intelligent hypothesis. When I ask why the balloon is inflated I am regularly told that it's because hot air rises. I then raise the hypothesis: 'What would happen if I hold the balloon-covered bottle upside down as I heat it?' The general response is that the balloon would not inflate. Some even speculate that the hot air rising would suck the balloon up in. I would hope that by this stage the suggestions of falsity are no longer necessary, that the intrinsic interest in the confirmation or disconfirmation of their hypothesis is sufficient. The majority who have opted for the non-inflating hypothesis are astonished to see the balloon inflate just as before. They are forced by their own intelligence and experience to the better explanation that the air would like to go up but that as there is no way up through hard glass, it has to go down, pushing soft rubber. The concept of expansion is thriving.

What is crucial is not how long false claims are presented or suggested, but whether the children are learning not to rely upon teacher's clues and responses as to what the right answer is, or is thought to be. As I argue in Chapter 8, children must somehow be disorientated from such reliance. My falsity strategy is one clear way of doing this.

I have produced a professional video, *Magic, Science and Critical Thinking; Sir, Can I Disagree With You?* to demonstrate and to argue and be argued with on this pedagogic strategy. The video shows three stages of exploration; my very aggressive defence of my magic and superior knowledge based on book learning and 'having been to college', leading to the children's successful challenge; secondly my more subtle attempts to manipulate them to the view that children should be seen and not heard; finally my debriefing on the experience. Teaching of ethnic-Asian eleven-year-olds is interspersed with responses and quite hostile questioning from SAPERE AGM, and with reflections from the class teacher, from CT specialists and from me on my approach and the children's responses.

In history and geography there is no problem in introducing children to the delights of falsity, without teacher complicity. I was about fourteen before I heard the idea that a text book could be wrong. I was shocked but convinced as a classmate told the teacher that 'that was not the way ye cut turf, leastwise not by the Loch.' He explained how he had seen and done it, in contradiction of the text book's declared sole method. Like Cocky Locky in the Swartz and Parks book, I believed him, but unlike Cocky Locky, I relished the plausibility and strength of his explanation.

Up-to-date history needs to deal similarly with falsity or, a form of it, contradiction. This is an area that has been developed in exciting ways by an imaginative American teacher, Kevin O'Reilly, used extensively by Swartz and Parks. O'Reilly presents, for example, one account of the outbreak of hostilities in the American War of Independence, from an eye-witness account by American insurgents, 'showing' that the British opened fire. When the students have relished this 'fact', he presents a British military 'intelligence' report which claims the opposite. When this contradiction has been savoured and processed, he moves to historians' accounts, representing the same perspectives and contradiction (the British source being Winston Churchill). This material is so good that it is worth using just to develop scepticism about sources, long before it is academically or intellectually appropriate to introduce children to such American history. But a history co-ordinator will supply contradicting sources for the topics you deal with.

The topic can be brought up to date with contradictory claims of a different professional sort, though still historical. John Hinckley was accused and convicted of the shooting of President Reagan. Present to your class the following statement, made for the prosecution or defence. Ask if they think it is relevant in a court of law, and attend closely to how they treat it. If they don't know the words 'psychiatric' and 'psychotic', the eleven-year-olds who watch that sort of television, or you, can explain. The statement is:

> It is a psychiatric fact that Mr Hinckley was psychotic.
>
> (Dr David M. Bear)

When this has been processed, and their view of both its relevance and its truth assessed, present them with this statement:

> Mr Hinckley has not been psychotic at any time.
>
> (Dr Park E. Dietz)

These examples are taken from a book that I would recommend to anyone who wanted to develop personal critical thinking. Moore and Parker's *Critical Thinking*, 1992, has an excellent combination of real examples and sound treatment, presenting advanced material which I have found very suitable for top juniors.

Falsity in geography is even easier to set up. Consider a question such as the population of a rapidly growing country like Australia. Give half the class one source in the library. My dated source at home, *Everyman's Encyclopaedia*, gives the population as 11,312,577. Give the other half of the class a different source, more up to date. The debate is usefully delayed and developed so that it is accuracy of sources and complex truth that win the argument, rather than one half of the class over the other.

I was asked for help once by a friend who was struggling to teach the water cycle to eight-year-olds, and had got into a rut of right-answer responses: 'cloud', 'river', 'evaporation', etc. I took a group of seven and asked them a trick question:

> If I went down to the river in Holmfirth and filled a glass with water from the river, how long would it be before I could go back and fill it with the same water when the cycle was complete?

A boy said a year; a girl said never. Another boy said at least a hundred years. We listened for the seven minutes it took for them to agree that it would never happen. As they talked and listened, they dealt with complex concepts such as dispersal, chance, mingling, terrain variables, the smallest unit and criterion of sameness. So they dealt with concepts that they could not possibly deal with using precise, academic words. They also talked about funny questions.

They were right. Mine was a funny question. It was not 'teacherly'. My odd question was not an academic but an intellectual invitation, and their response was delightful and intellectual, rather than academic. Their tongues and ears had been loosened and released from the right-answer cycle, and they had experienced the excitement of ideas, their own ideas.

That last example might be considered to belong to a variety of subjects. I would make a special plea that media studies be subjected to the falsity approach. There is so much that is presented with superficial but compelling skill in the media, that we should be alarmed by our failure to counteract it. Sometimes it is a matter of pointing out falsity, though that is not easy against the authority of the printed word. I once quite failed to get a Year 5 class to agree that there was a journalist's error in a Sun editorial which quoted 'a brilliant 32-word sentence by Mrs Thatcher'. It contained 33 words. Their explanations were worryingly intelligent, considering their underlying motivation.

Thatcher brings me to an example and in turn to a more general point. The example is a statement she has often used, along with politicians of all parties, when asked an awkward question that puts them on the spot. The response is the imperious and learned-sounding:

I never answer hypothetical questions.

This is usually said condescendingly, as if the interviewer ought to have known better than to have asked it. Most eleven-year-olds can easily come to see that this means the politician would never reveal what they would do if they were to win the next election, or what they would do if they were to answer constructively any 'if' question. One hardly needs to prepare with contradictory evidence to such a claim, since it is so abundant in the newspapers. And the best method is when the children are obliged to search the papers themselves, learning to identify the offending contradictions, the falsehoods.

The children must learn the word 'hypothetical', which is within the grasp of the average nine-year-old. It is astonishing that it is in mathematics, in areas which have little application to our lives, that children learn so many complex Latin and Greek words, but in logic, words that apply to so many of our sentences are not learned, with the consequent loss of control of vital thinking. 'Hypothetical', 'necessary' and 'contradiction' are examples of such words.

When children from nine years up have had the early part of the 'contradiction' lesson detailed in Chapter 2 they are capable of playing more complex games of truth, falsity, possibility, contradiction and necessary truth. It is valuable for them to play these games and to construct such games, based on their own commonsense experience. They can make up necessarily true sets of statements, necessarily false ones and contingently true ones (it all depends). These can be applied to real-life statements where people try to get away with the appearance of wisdom. Statements such as 'I don't think we should be unduly concerned about that development' and 'My own opinion is that an over-reaction would not be appropriate at the present time' are not what they seem to be. They are not recommendations, despite appearance. They are necessary truths, tautologies, dressed up as 'sound judgement'. A grasp of the status of such sentences is so much easier when children can see the symmetry of necessary truth and contradiction.

This point allows me to give the major reason, beyond fun, motivation etc, for my deep concern with falsity. It is the better to appreciate the truth. Just as the person who has a deep understanding of evil has a deepened understanding of the good, so familiarity with falsity establishes a context for the true. There are many natural dispositions in us, I believe, which urge us towards the truth, though not necessarily towards truth telling. There is the curiosity so abundant in the child from six months onwards. There is the search for regularity which drives us to distraction when we encounter the discrepant, or what I term 'recalcitrant experience'. There are the tendencies celebrated by Piaget, of accommodating new experience, and the generative state of disequilibration.

These tendencies are powerful on their own, particularly in the lucky child whose education has proceeded along the lines of the development of curiosity. But they are not often greatly activated by the teacher providing further truths to set alongside prior truths. At times, I argue, it is better to confront the peaceful truth with fractious falsehood, in the guise of authority. It is better to create an energetic uncertainty, to provoke disequilibrium, even at the expense of the teacher's paradoxically deserting the bounden duty of defending the emblem of truth seeking. The end of intellectual growth richly justifies the means.

Chapter 7

An experience of INSET

An interesting way of tying up some of the lesson-based ideas in this book is to give some detail of a day's INSET in a school, with a substantial focus on the reactions of the staff to observing me working with their children (for the first time), to their pursuing the ideas with other classes and their reactions, and to my twilight inputs on the day of the teaching and the day before. It may be specially helpful because I used lessons outlined here, so the teachers' reactions may be similar or indeed interestingly different from yours in reflection or in practice.

The background to the day was that in 1995 the Tyneside TEC funded a project on teaching thinking skills in Britain. The project was based in Newcastle University's Education Department, and the project director, Dr Vivienne Baumfield, came to observe me working in a primary school, as one of five case studies of practitioners. For the launch of the report, *Improving Students' Performance: A Guide to Thinking Skills Programmes in Education and Training*, I was invited by the University to provide a workshop for interested teachers and academics. One of those attending the workshop was Sue Duncan, an advisor with Newcastle Education Authority, who was enthused by the ideas and in turn invited me to join Newcastle's Director of Education, David Bell, to lead a workshop with the Newcastle middle school heads and deputies. This led to one of the heads asking me to do a day's INSET in his school, Throckley Middle, in September, 1996. The day was one of great fun and was well caught by Tyne-Tees Television, who broadcast the 'Critical Thinking in Science' lesson in their region.

I asked the head, Mike Routledge, if he and the teachers would be prepared to co-operate in the case study. They agreed and he sent me the following statement:

Critical Thinking: The School Perspective

Through a framework of self review Throckley is striving to raise standards particularly in terms of pupil achievement. Curriculum development and innovation are essential to ensure a curriculum and pedagogy which is relevant to the needs of young people and allows them to realise their full potential. To enable teachers to achieve this, a section of the school development plan is explicitly focused on supporting the broadening and development of effective teaching and learning approaches.

An identified problem in school was an aspect of under-achievement in speaking and listening which related to classroom discussion and was characterised by pupils who exhibited the following features:

low self-esteem
limited skills of social interaction
an inability to transfer skills across subjects

In response to common cries from teachers which included 'I wish s/he would think before s/he opens her/his mouth' and 'So-and-so never says anything . . . even when they know the answer', the school began looking for a solution.

I had been involved in problem solving in outdoor education with the emphasis on articulating the process of solution rather than simply stating an answer. Having read articles on critical thinking by Dr Victor Quinn and then having the opportunity to listen and talk with him at a day conference the idea of using this approach to solve the problem relating to classroom discussion was sown and a course of action built into the school development plan.

Having seen the strategy demonstrated with their own classes and having developed some of the techniques used as part of their own teaching, staff are unanimous in their view that it has tremendous potential to create situations and tasks which encourage pupils to think hard and articulate their thoughts. As a result further time will be devoted to its development under Dr Quinn's guidance.

After my teaching he wrote, outlining developments he would like to see, arising from the experience.

Enclosed are four uncensored responses from teachers observing your sessions. Carol Strickson has also included some language recorded in writing during one of the Year 5 sessions.

Everyone is keen to continue development and contact with yourself. The question is how? I wondered if a return visit structured to meet specific needs might be useful. One-to-one sessions with Paul, Angela and Carol might be possible and Ruth Affleck is keen for you to work with her class for a longer period of time. Funding for a return could be found but all of us would value some kind of long term project and this is more difficult to resource.

Finally can I say that as the head I am very keen not to lose momentum on this development. It had a big impact and a positive one. Your thoughts on how to progress in the light of the above comments would be most welcome.

In previous INSET work I had often asked for and received feedback, but I had never had such valuable material. Feedback is often rushed and may be resented, coming at a time when teachers are keen to go home. This feedback was relaxed and thoughtful. I present the feedback from Angela Gemmell, identifying the most useful issues it raised for me and comments I would like to highlight, and I respond to a number of issues.

I enjoyed observing the lesson and found it worthwhile to watch different techniques to draw more lengthy and meaningful responses from the children. I noted particularly the technique of leading the children to explain what they meant by saying 'And so . . .?'

In a short while the children were doing this themselves without the prompting. Examples of contradictions were familiar and therefore meaningful to the children like 'In a universe with no water there was an orange.' 'Red herrings' created discussion between the children like 'In a universe there were no bricks and I passed a house.'

Pace was slow but I felt this was appropriate when dealing with an unfamiliar class who had probably never experienced this type of activity. I thought it was important that the less able ones were given time to take in what was being asked of them.

I found the final contradiction of the lesson most thought provoking, and was impressed with the quality of the children's responses. 'There was once a universe with no language and the girl thought to herself . . .' provoked the response: 'You said in a universe there was not language so she could not think to herself because she would be thinking in language,' from Mark. James replied to this with the fact that she could be thinking of a picture and would not need words. Other children kept saying that it was impossible to picture something if you did not know the word for it. Two children said you could picture your home, or yourself, which I found extremely interesting.

On the whole, the activity gave me a lot of techniques to think about and experiment with. It was refreshing to see the importance given to a 'thinking' lesson and the fact that no writing was involved. I think that perhaps a shorter block of time would have kept the children's interest more, but appreciate that the hour was used to show teachers the full range of techniques.

I tried the same lesson with a Year 7 English class with much of the same responses. They could all give me examples of contradictions by the end of the lesson: I spent a shorter amount of time on the the simple contradictions, moving quickly on to the more challenging ones. I asked the class to think of contradictions for a 15 year old, and received some high-level responses. For example: 'There was once a universe with no gravity and I went sailing in a boat.'

The discussion about thought without language was more prolonged and there was a lot of disagreement between four or five children. Two of the girls became very intense insisting that you could not think of something if you did not know the word for it.

I am keen to follow up this discussion with a similar quality activity, but am not sure where to go next. A third of the children in the Year 7 class had switched off towards the end of the lesson and I would like to have suggestions for keeping their interest; how could a lesson like this be differentiated?

The issues and comments her kind letter raises for me are:

● pacing
● the separate treatment of critical thinking
● less able children's need for more time to think
● moving to not needing prompting to explain
● novelty of experience
● value of shorter time
● shorter time on simple contradictions
● one third had switched off towards the end, when she tried it.

I put pacing first because her letter and, even more strongly, Paul Tankard's (below) make the point. Fortunately this is the most highly adaptable feature of many lessons. Had I been watching, and familiar with the class, I would almost certainly spot the times when it needed a change of pace, particularly for the less conspicuous children. At the same time, I agree with Angela's point about the value of a slower pace, as I have argued a number of times, so long as the delicate balance of differentiated motivation is retained. The concept of contradiction makes hugely deeper intrusions into our general consciousness and conversation than do most of the maths concepts we learn, such as 'rectangular'. But also, with a concept as rich as 'contradiction', developed through children-led examples, I prefer to go with the lower half's or third's pace, because there is such scope for the brighter children to make elaborate examples, and more of them. A final point is that the simpler examples seem insignificant by comparison with the philosophical learning about the dependence of language on thought, but from a logical rather than philosophical point of view, the simpler examples are sufficient to develop competence.

With regard to Angela's question about differentiation, apart from what I have already said, I would urge more group work, where the groups are if necessary given examples to work on. With some children it is a new experience to be asked to be creative outside the arts. Of course we must shock that culture, but not at the expense of frustrated children. Providing existing examples, including other children's, at least takes this group out of the drop-outs, and if the examples are of varied complexity, this does much more.

I do value Angela's point about the children moving to not needing the prompt I start them with. This relates to a number of fundamental points. It relates to the need for the questioning stimulus to move from the teacher to the learner. It relates to the critical apprenticeship approach. And it relates to the general value of nurturing autonomy.

Finally I valued her point about the importance of *familiar* examples. Her own work gives a good illustration of this:

> There was once a universe with no gravity and I went sailing in a boat.

The importance of the familiar relates, in my mind, to the importance of the intellectual rather than the academic: the gravity quotation is intellectually delightful, but where does it belong, academically? Not even in physics. It relates too to the likelihood of transfer to children's general thinking about their lives.

With regard to her point about a quality follow-up activity, there is a range of things in the chapter on falsity. Within a single week recently I taught two lessons to Year 7 classes, devoted entirely to 'Funny Sentences'. I began by asking them to write false sentences. When we had heard everyone's, I asked them to discuss whether their sentence could be true, or would always be false. When the culture shock of this question wore off, they had no difficulty in facing it. There were easy cases like 'There is a thunderstorm.' More difficulties arose with 'My Dad's car is a moped', and there were difficulties even with 'A wheel is a square' (to do with original designs and also the arbitrariness of language). My thinking in seeing these as follow-up is that the idea of positive and negative necessity is raised. There is much scope for the children to explore the contrast between the conceptual and the empirical, even if as with both these classes, no previous work had been done on it and the terms were not introduced.

Paul Tankard's comments were based on observation of the same lesson but mostly consist of very interesting report and comment on his own progressing of the ideas. He writes:

I enjoyed watching Victor's lesson with 6AG in which he developed the children's ORAL and THINKING skills through a discussion of 'contradiction'. Victor's teaching style and subtle forms of discipline were impressive and I was surprised by the level of cognitive processes demonstrated by the majority of these Year 6 pupils. Though I feel the pace of the lesson was a little slow and the concept of 'contradiction' reinforced longer than necessary, I feel that I, and perhaps many teachers, rush lessons (for varying reasons) and certainly the aim of Victor's session was achieved. It is likely that these Year 6 pupils could still quickly provide good personal examples of 'contradiction'. In the long term deep understanding of a smaller number of concepts/skills might be more worthwhile than a superficial knowledge of many concepts retained for short spells. While I have much experience of developing children's oral skills and have tried out many 'problem-solving' activities with children aged 7–10, I nevertheless gained a great deal from observing Victor's lesson. His useful list of 'Educative Questioning' will be employed by me in future English lessons.

The 'contradictory' activity has been carried out with two of my English classes (Years 7 & 8) and similar responses were made by the children to those in 6AG. Of course, the older pupils grasped the concept at a quicker rate and I was impressed by the children's own examples of 'contradiction' and level of thought when discussing the question 'Can we think without language?'

This latter part of both lessons was stimulating and many children were keen to pursue this philosophical line, e.g.:

a) Can a hungry baby 'think/picture' a bottle feed without knowing the word(s)?

b) Can children 'think' of their school lunch at 11.00 am without 'thinking' of the words on the canteen menu?

The lesson concluded with a discussion of basic semantics and how humans perceive reality through the five senses, e.g.:

a) How can you prove a pen is a pen?

b) How can you prove that you are a pupil at Throckley Middle School?

A possible alien view of Earth and its features by a creature with x-ray vision, telepathic powers and an owl's hearing range was discussed at quite a profound level and I was surprised at a sizeable minority (about 30%) of these 11 to 13 year olds pursuing such 'critical thinking' with enthusiasm and astonishing insight. The possibilities of such a line of 'critical thinking' are fascinating and the children and I would certainly benefit from a repeat visit by Victor and staff discussion on how Throckley Middle School could develop a module of 'oral skills' in this area.

The features and issues I highlight are:

- level of cognitive processes demonstrated
- pace too slow (again)
- importance of deep understanding
- developing a module of oral skill in this area.

What is most encouraging about Angela's and Paul's responses is that they both tried the idea, fine-tuned it for pace, and it worked for them both. This is encouraging because I am often told that my ideas are too dependent on my personality. In fact what my ideas are dependent on is the raising of appropriate intellectual expectations. This book is an outline of how to do that, and these teachers' success is confirmation of that possibility and fact. There is in their work the same vigour of example: 'thinking of school lunch, without the menu words, at 11.00 am'. There is a willingness to be surprised by the level of cognitive process and to accept the challenge of pursuing deeper understanding to the extent of Paul's seeing the children's 'enthusiasm and astonishing insight' when he tried the ideas.

With regard to a module of oral skill in this area, I hope that Paul will be pleased with the ideas I have assembled here. The module would be like a graph, with two axes. One indicates the range of lessons that work, along with follow-up lessons, while the other indicates the skills that are being developed. These skills are those of argument, of distinction, of questioning, of imagining critically, of general and specific intellectual virtue. In short, they are the skills of critical thinking as I have here conceived and presented it.

The third response from Throckley was from Kay Hallowell on the science lesson that was televised.

Dr Victor Quinn's visit to Throckley Middle School, 18 September 1996
Periods 3/4, Year 7D, 12 year old children, 15 in group, boys/girls
LESSON: Cool Air Contracts/Hot Air Expands

This group of 12 year olds were selected because of their specific Technology needs and they had the pleasure, on this day, of a Science lesson. A common need of the pupils in this group is to extend their concentration span.

After introductions, but not to the TV staff, pupils were happy and relaxed to be 'taken over' by Dr Quinn. They coped extremely well with a quick change-over from their teacher to a stranger. At the same time the pupils were aware that staff, known and unknown, were present in the room, soon to be forgotten because a friendly, calm and quiet voice addressed them; an invitation to take part in a stunning 'magic trick' captivating each pupil. Concentration was to last throughout the lesson. Bells rang for change of lesson and lunch time. No one moved, not out of courtesy, but out of real and genuine interest for the on-going experiment. Participation of each pupil, ensured by Dr Quinn, seemed to give a one-to-one involvement to each pupil, even though they were within a group situation. The practical/visual demonstration along with the speaking and listening was a bonus: eyes, ears and an opportunity to be heard.

I found the exercise beneficial

- take time, slow down a lesson for better pupil involvement and perhaps better understanding
- pupils who usually lack concentration by

  - moving head from side to side
  - having tight shoulders
  - fidgeting

actually remained quite still and relaxed – even though the pupils' seats are uncomfortable over long periods of time.

Kay's comments have little criticism, but she does catch some points that I consider important. A point not specially to do with critical thinking is the power of voice in setting tone. I have heard even drama teachers using an authoritative voice when there were no problems of control and when exactly what was needed was a soft, enticing, conspiratorial voice. The power of voice as the instrument of control can hardly be overstated.

She also draws attention to the importance of retaining interest. I was using surprise to a great extent, and the surprise was based on setting up (usually false) expectations, where the expectations were rejected by the empirical evidence. I must admit, though, that she is too kind to me regarding the chairs they sat on. With hindsight I should have arranged some reason for a move round on a few occasions, just to relieve the strain of limbs, from the high stools.

The final report is from Carol Strickson on the lesson 'What is the world?' She writes:

I enjoyed watching Victor with the children and the children certainly enjoyed the time that he spent with them.

Victor made it all look so easy and if we hope to achieve a similar standard (a tall order) then we really need much more guidance and input. Ideas need to be discussed as to how we can use this approach in our classroom within the context of the curriculum – or should we approach it as a separate entity – another question to be answered!

The session after school could maybe have been more useful if we had discussed this area rather than just recapping each lesson.

Pupil responses from Year 5 to the lesson 'What is the World?'

You could not play football because you could not hold on to it and pick it up because you would not have anything to stand on.

You could not play football with the world on the field because the field is part of the world.

If the tractor was on the world how are you meant to play football?

If you dug up the field and if you put it in a separate place with the digger and you were playing football, the tractor and field would go down because they are in mid-air.

If you go down, where do you go down to?

If there is no gravity in space, then you would not go down, you would just float.

When Hollie said there was a planet underneath you, there cannot be two planets on one world.

Carol's report contains energetic statements which usefully show the syntactic complexity of children's speech, in circumstances such as these. Each of the seven statements above is a compound sentence either of causal relation or of condition. The fourth is a brilliant one of three consecutive conditionals followed by an entailment drawn from these, which in turn is accurately supported by an entailed causal clause. It is statements like these, however complicated my description of them may make them seem, that make me wonder how much experience of teaching the devisers of the NC can have had when they thought it wise for children to start using in their speech some of the sophisticated syntax characteristic of their writing. If children are properly questioned and listened to, it is precisely the reverse process that is important. It is their writing that needs to take on some of the complexity of their real, thoughtful speech, if only we can reveal and capture it. Carol has captured it here.

She asks a crucial and poignant question: 'Should the approach be through the general curriculum or through a separate subject?' I have no hesitation in saying that it should be both. As the schooling crises of 1996 progressed there seemed to be a mood reflected by SCAA that critical thinking should be a subject, taught and examined like others. The important points are twofold, in my opinion. First, there are many teachers at present who will not and should not be so patient as to await that great time. The task is too important to be put off, and there is much that teachers can do now, in the primary class with their own children, and in the secondary with their own subjects. Secondly, Carol's intimation is right that there should be a separate entity, critical thinking. It is like English across the curriculum. Every teacher is a teacher of English, and should know how to do it in relation to their own subject. But there should be a subject co-ordinator who has a special responsibility and competence in the area, to help at least those who seek help.

PART B

Process

Chapter 8

Educative questioning

In a sense, this book is about the role of questioning in the quality activation of young minds. One might then ask what a second chapter on questioning is doing since questioning is such a pervasive feature. I have made clear that quality teaching is largely quality questioning and the chapter draws attention, not to questioning in context, as the others do, but to the range of questions that characterise an intellectually healthy classroom.

I begin with some points from research: boys are asked and answer many more questions than girls, by male and female teachers; delay after a question is important, as argued earlier; pseudo-questions (answers known) predominate; convergent, recall questions predominate, even in arts areas. Shallow-end predominance means restriction from intellectual-sensory-imaginative-appreciative development.

I want to delay with this point about shallow-end, also known as 'right-answer', questions. They predominate to a worrying extent, and far beyond the requirements of the NC. They tend to define education in a child's mind as the transfer of information from the teacher's into the children's minds. In one breath we deride this with Dickensian images but in another we scrupulously adhere to it for reasons that must be very deep in many of us, perhaps to do with professional security and the insecurity of the uncertain. I wonder how it is that between the mid-eighties and the mid-nineties the word 'deliver' became the predominant verb and metaphor for teaching, with all its baggage of one-way transactions and its antipathy to developing. I suspect again that it is its ability to bolster security. But if it is accepted, it is clear that the role of questioning is the shallow one that confirms delivery. Important questions, on this model, are questions whose answers confirm that the information has been received, the message delivered.

The taxonomy that I present is a mixture of psychological and logical types. It is intended not to replace closed questions, but to go alongside them in order to make a much richer experience of education. In each case I give a brief characterisation and an example of the type:

- *Zoom-in* questions invite a closer look: How many legs has it?
- *Zoom-out* questions ask for connections with your life: Do you know any like it?
- *Evaluative (moral)* questions ask for a moral response: Should we eat dead cows' flesh?
- *Evaluative (aesthetic)* questions ask for a felt appreciation or judgement: Which picture do you like best?
- *Predictive* questions ask about the future: What will happen when we put it in warm water?
- *Hypothetical* questions operate in the conditional: What would a bully feel after a lesson on experiences of being bullied?
- *Explanatory* questions ask to make sense of things: Why do we have pets?
- *Conceptual* questions ask what words or signs mean: What is a ghost?
- *Philosophical* questions are second-order: If there was no language would it be possible to think?
- *Analytical* questions ask for distinctions: Is litter the same as pollution?
- *Technical* questions ask how processes work: How do clouds vanish?
- *Logical* questions ask about follow-on connections between ideas: If you say 'Children should be seen and not heard', why do you listen to us when we disagree with you?
- *Applied* questions ask about implementation or application: How do you increase the chances of children taking their classroom learning of critical thinking into their general experience of the media etc?

Some categories overlap. It is important that none be left out. Think too of other categories that are important.

Don't be misled by appearances. 'What is a home?' could be an open-ended conceptual zoom-out question. The teacher's behaviour might make clear, however, that there is one right answer: 'A place of human habitation'. Such behaviour is common. We must not assume that it is the work of idiots. We all do it and mostly don't catch ourselves doing it.

A good way to develop skill in the range of questioning is to make questions in each category, in an area of personal interest. When this is easy, go to your classroom display and think of a range of questions that might feature in the display. These are intended to get children thinking, in front of the display. This is useful as an easy first step, as the writing is at your own pace, and you can note effectiveness as children work in groups on the display. Once you have a ready facility here, move to an oral exchange with children. Start with a story and prepared questions. Finally work without prepared questions, developing the tip-of-the-tongue facility, so that your taxonomy is only occasionally referred to, to check. Your proper objects of consciousness are your topic and children, not your list of questions.

Two things can help: a friend learning with you, to talk your progress through, and a recorder (audio or video) to let you see what you are doing right and wrong. Listen with a (good!) friend. Most of us are surprised to learn the extent of our unintended insensitivity, if we really listen and if we have truly generous criteria as to how we should listen.

The initial focus is on you as questioner. It must change to creating a climate where such questions are natural, coming from children. Devote a lesson to questioning as I have suggested in the other questioning chapter. Have a box for written ones, or a speaking and listening period, with plenary and group times. An OHP or flip-chart can register their questions; the important points can be reinforced that articulating the question is an achievement, and questions are not just things to which there are right answers if only you're clever enough to know them. Children must be disabused of a great deal on this topic.

I have regularly taught INSET sessions based on this material. My usual pattern has been to teach a number of short lessons, observed by the teachers, followed by a twilight session. In the twilight work I try to demystify the process. Having seen the children work with me helps, but I need to draw out the particular questions and types of questions with the teachers. Then we follow the process I indicated above of a workshop on constructing questions. Finally we stand in front of a display making real questions we think suitable for their class. Apart from vocabulary, it is very interesting how little difference age makes. Of course the outcomes are age-differentiated, but the appropriate questions for seven- and twelve-year-olds are often the same: the question 'Which picture has the best backing?', in a display, may draw no response from children unused to such a question, but will do equally for the divergent ages, when they are used to them.

I do put in some more advanced points for some teachers to push themselves beyond the basic achievement. As you might expect, the idea of meta-questioning usually features. When I am asked to return to the school, I look for deep developments of the work. Imagine my delight when one such school/teacher had a display in a corridor where the photographs were separated from the questions. The display title featured this, with the question 'Can you tell which set of questions goes with which photo?' So this meta-question had to be answered before the subordinate (and themselves delightfully ranged) questions could be approached. The challenge of the meta-question, the teacher told me, had great effect in drawing in casual passers-by.

Perhaps the most important point about questioning, which I will develop in the chapter on climate, is that the classroom should be characterised by enquiry, by curiosity, by inquisitiveness, by wonder, rather than by ritual questioning, by inquisition, or by 'second-hand' questioning. The classroom should be a place of research, with the emphasis not on *re*search, but on re*search*. When I take a class for the first time, children start at a loss because of my 'unteacherly' manner. They wonder at my wondering and saying 'I wonder . . .' or 'I'll need a minute to think about that' or just my silence as I do think. Our paralanguage, well explained by David Wood (1997), is crucial in letting children see the importance we attach to the questioning, reflective attitude.

Chapter 9
The social intellectual virtues

This title may sound rather grand for something that is as simple as the ground-rules of good discussion in your classroom. It is more grand because these features of discussion and in particular of argument are more than customs to be established. They are constitutive of the good intellectual life in company with those who wish to explore the quality of their beliefs. Their absence in so many discussions even among educated adults is a reason to believe that we need to take more seriously in schools the task of establishing them for what they really are: not just ground-rules, but the hallmark of a real social, intellectual engagement.

You are familiar with the normal idea of virtue and vice. It is based on respect for others, in that others have interests, needs and rights that we must not over-ride. Thus bullying, cheating and lying offend against moral virtue.

Intellectual virtue, however, is based on how we ought to behave with others, from the point of view not of their rights as persons, but of our both wishing to improve the quality of our beliefs. It is seeking truth, seeking more critically defensible views, or just learning from each other. I add the word 'social' to distinguish my concern from other intellectual virtues of a more solitary sort, such as perseverance, checking sources and scrupulousness. Many of us have much to learn, to approach this social state.

A good starting point is my pervasive concern with challenging the tabloid culture. A feature of this culture is the over-riding tendency to deal in conclusions rather than in approaching and examining ideas. It can be represented as a personal weakness if, in relation to any topic, a conclusion is not available immediately. Hesitation, or the need to think, are signs of this weakness, in many conversations. I don't know how difficult it would be to reverse this tendency, but since the reversal has not seriously been tried, like so many ideas put forward in this book, I am sure that it is too early to be pessimistic.

Another starting point is an adult one. When I sit back and listen to a conversation even among educated people, I am often struck by recurring pattern. It is not a dialogue in the rich sense of that word, but is serial monologues. Four people drinking coffee have a common topic and they stick to the point but none of them refers, except as self-introduction, to what others have said. There is no questioning or exploration; there is no appreciation or qualification; there is telling, telling, telling. Like old folk on the bus telling of their ailments, each has a tape to play and there is impatience with each of the others that they take too long and don't even leave a plausible, interruptible pause. There must be in most of us a desire to tell, that is independent of the desire that ideally accompanies telling, that we be appreciatively listened to.

If this is as common as I believe it is, we must work on ourselves as well as our children. It is easy, as I said, to hear this feature in an eavesdropped conversation, or if I distance myself from my own group's conversation. As with moral virtues, so with intellectual, how do I become not just familiar with them, but a practitioner? One way is to discover the tapes in one's memory that one so wants to play, even when no-one is really listening. I can only do that by catching myself at it. It is difficult, as is doing something about it, which I will indicate when I deal with decentring. (See also my postscript to this chapter.)

Some of my recommendations relate to our responsibilities to children, some to ourselves. In this as in so many things we are all learners. But the scope for modelling good behaviour in this area is so great that combined with the difficulty of my getting knowledge about myself, I and we should be humbled into great diligence to know and improve ourselves.

Say your bit

There is a quality even more fundamental than the truth in your ideas, and that is that they are your ideas. You owe it to the group that the ideas be heard. They deserve to have their go, to have their chance in the world and their chance in our group. So whatever reluctance there is on your part to contribute to the group, and for whatever reason, it must be overcome, for your sake and for the ideas' sake. Do not feel exonerated by the fact that you can gain much from a discussion by just listening. Others should be able to benefit from you as you can from them. What sort of group member and colleague are you if you not only don't but can't readily put your views and experience to a group? I remember the reluctance I had, and overcoming it.

This does nothing to diminish your right to silence and to secrecy. But beyond these, the enormity of the task must not be avoided. The reasons for silence, if I can mix a metaphor, have murky roots. They have a lot to do with other aspects dealt with in this chapter, with failure, rejection, intimidation and the implanting of low self-expectation. So they have a lot to do with bullying in the home, the peer-group and the classroom. To expect a child to 'snap out of it' is generally unreasonable. Overcoming it has much to do with the provision for the child of appropriate social tasks, of preparation for each task and of support and praise in the performance. An example with literate children is to ask them to remember a time when they were afraid. Ask them to write something down, to remind them. You know in your class the reticent individuals to check, and the prompting questions: 'Were you ever afraid that your pet might die?', '. . . of the dark?' With something written in front of them, the task of breaking the silence is less daunting.

On the other hand there often are young children who for whatever reason never put a hand up in response to a question. Games can be useful. I have tried 'Hands up how many of you have got a name,' and 'Are there any windows in this room?' True, these are odd points, but these and others, delivered with a wait until every hand is up, do represent a breakthrough with a certain kind of child.

Talk in moderation

This clearly doesn't contradict the previous point: the opposite extreme should be avoided. Confident and articulate people risk talking too much. One can offend by making excessively long contributions to discussion, or by making too many contributions when others would or might like to contribute. A lengthy contribution in talk is usually a very different experience for speaker and listener. The speaker brings relived images, props, emotions and a range of tacit understandings to the exchange. These are in her head, not the listener's. We should know this but we are not taught it. If we are confident socially, we often talk too much, and are unaware that we do so. There is in many of us a deep-seated belief that an experience or idea gains a particular importance by virtue of its being *our* experience or idea. This belief is less in evidence in children, though many of them talk too much. They should encounter it and learn to guard against it.

Decentring is a vital idea. It is the achievement whereby I learn what it is that you need to hear or experience in order to share what is in my mind, whether it be a question, an idea or a supportive anecdote. It is very difficult, and the difficulty is generally not broached in school. When children have learned to give and receive criticism constructively, they can be invited to comment on others' contributions to discussion. This has the enormous advantage that it is 'the other' who can most help me out of egocentricity, whether it be the egocentricity of too much talk, or of my next item, a lack of conciseness. David Wood's chapter 'Making sense' (Wood 1997) is an excellent treatment of decentring, more general than mine. He gives telling evidence for the egocentric view that:

> Being relatively inexperienced and lacking expertise in the task of analysing and evaluating their own and other people's verbal communication, most young children assume that failures of communication are necessarily the fault of whoever is listening.

This central idea of my book, decentring, could come at many places. I put it here, between the 'moderation' and the 'economy' points, to draw attention to its enormous importance in developing knowledge about self in conversation. Just as critical thinking is thinking with appropriate care, decentred performance is social performance with appropriately caring self-knowledge. It requires the ability to stand five paces behind the classroom chair on which I sit and to contribute with my classmates whilst simultaneously listening to myself critically and consequently amending my contributions. It is so easy to learn to note the weaknesses of my classmates. My own elude all but the strictest self-scrutiny, but if I have a teacher who can intervene in the right way, it becomes a great deal easier at least to recognise instances. Recognising patterns is then also made easier.

I make one further point about decentring. Strictly, in this context, it has to do with examining quality of beliefs, but I took it more generally for two reasons. One is that it is a human excellence of great and general importance. The other is that some children and some adults are so attached to their beliefs and attitudes, beyond rational warrant, that it is easier for them to learn to decentre in discussions where defending one's position is not involved. It is easier for all of us to learn about self, about economy in contribution, about listening well and so forth, if we are doing something simple like exploring the experiences.

Be economical, be concise

Try to plan what you are going to say. Put communication before expression. People will listen to you better, or should, if you are as brief as your message can be. The enemies of this point are twofold. One is the tendency not to think that a contribution needs a definite end and, having made the point, to just carry on talking because the floor is yours until you stumble on to an embarrassed end. Your point can easily be missed by this degeneration. The second enemy is the tendency to make a perfectly good point, clearly, and then carry on making the same point in slightly different words, as repetition that is mindless rather than well-judged. Think in advance what you are going to say and how best you can say it, to save people effort and boredom. I often, in a thoughtful discussion, use the opportunity to develop the point about giving and receiving criticism. I ask if the previous speaker would like his or her point summarised, leaving out nothing important. Others or I are prepared to do so, and to consider the advantages of the longer and shorter versions. I have also used recorded (thoughtless, local radio) phone-ins, to alert children to the huge lack of economy and planning on the part of people who knew they were about to speak. This exercise is also great fun as the children see obvious weakness of contribution, even though the remediation is more difficult than they can understand. At least the object of aspiration is there.

Encourage the reticent

There is potential conflict with the previous point. Those having difficulty with an idea or emerging from psychological silence deserve special consideration and should be identified by all group members, and encouraged. This point is similar to the first, but now the focus of responsibility is less on the teacher and individual than on the peers. Where two people begin to speak simultaneously, the more loquacious (who should know himself as such) should give way. In small groups, this is a special responsibility and I like to ensure that each group has an individual charged with it.

Tolerate a silence

A silence in discussion is not an embarrassment to be obscured by talk. It is an opportunity to gather courage and plan. Don't deny others that, by the imagined need to blot out a silence. A non-decentred person can easily fail to appreciate the constructive aspects of silence. I often require a period of silence after a question, 'thinking time', not just to allow thought, but to show that I value thought. I also often pause and visibly think appreciatively, before repeating the contribution, or asking for it to be repeated. We need silence and other strategies that slow down the proceedings and communicate reflectiveness.

Don't ridicule

Again, this is straightforward in theory; what is it in practice? It is important that you distinguish telling someone you think he is wrong from attempting to make a fool of him. The former is a vital step in the conduct of controversy (it invites evidence); the latter invites only unevidenced derision. Try to distinguish between making, and *scoring*, a point. Unlike some, this virtue is absolute.

If you take on this point, you are without doubt taking on the tabloid culture. So much of what takes place in the select committees, and on the floor of the Commons, in political debate in the media, is the desire to ridicule. By 'the media' I do not just mean the tabloid papers, nor do I mean only the politicians. The interviewing journalists normally have ridicule in their questions, which they defend, if challenged, by upholding their right to ask critical questions. They fail to make the elementary distinction between criticism and ridicule/derision. Politicians, journalists and virtually all controversialists behave thus, I am convinced, because they know that not enough of their listeners have been introduced to the distinction for it to be worth their while to feel constrained to avoid ridicule.

Avoid pejorative language

Within ridicule, I consider pejorative language the most potent instrument, so that I treat it separately. You must present your opponent's view as she would represent it. Regularly, people use pejorative words – 'whinge', 'quick fix', 'fad', 'bandy about' – to describe their opponent's view. They are condemning by description. It is unaccept-able because, worse than unhelpful, it is distracting; what should be questioned is whether what is objectively described is good or bad. To refer pejoratively, as opposed to descriptively, is clearly unfair. Such reference leads to timid compliance, angry retaliation or, ideally, logi-cal objection, each of which is a distraction from the point of sub-stance.

It is the device (or intellectual vice?) most widely drawn on by politicians, tabloid editorialists and journalists to catch the reader (without respect) by the scruff of the neck, and tell her what to think. If I were a politician, this is the learning I would most wish to keep from children, and from those who educate them. I would dread the consequences of their detecting what I was attempting. If schools taught this skill, then I as a politician would be bereft of my most manipulative device.

Don't interrupt

It follows from respecting and valuing others that we don't cut in on them. If someone is speaking to the group, it is distracting to engage in a chat with your neighbour. There are times when interruption may be correct: an escaped, stalking panther is circumstantially more important than an emerging distinction, however subtle. Interruptions in discussion far exceed such legitimacy. The requirement on the group member not to chatter or interrupt insensitively is matched by the right and duty of the teacher to ensure sensitively that such behav-iour is not condoned.

Don't aggress bodily

Non-verbal communication relates closely to intellectual virtue. We dismiss others not just by the words we use but by devices unavailable to editorialists. The paralinguistics of approval and dismissal are important. Are we conscious of how we use dismissive grins, a glance, shrug, rhetorical question or other signalled put-down? From the point of view of intellectual virtue, we must strive to distinguish animal aggression from rational engagement, not forgetting that whilst we are always animal, we are but sometimes rational.

Give and take criticism constructively

Present your disagreement in a positive way. Have your strength in evidence rather than conclusion. Try not to 'corner' the person. Suggest, if you can, a resolution, a proposed alternative, if your point is accepted. On the other side, open yourself to receiving criticism generously. Hear it out without interruption, impatience or dismissive gesture. You should never be uncritical of what you hear; the problem is that we don't allow ourselves the psychological freedom to hear critically what is said against us. Both in giving and receiving, we don't allow ourselves to see ourselves other than as the non-offending party.

As I have indicated, this is a skill that needs deliberate, not just incidental, attention. Thus the end of a composition lesson in music, visual art or creative writing can be designated just such an occasion. Attention is given to criticising the work, but subordinately to attention given to learning how to give and receive criticism. Eventually there is no subordinate, but only when there is much learning of the intellectual virtues.

Don't predispose in your questioning

Pejorative language is a major technique for letting the questioned child know what the approved answer is. In the following question, consider the difference in replacing the space by 'criticism' or 'whingeing'. 'Should we listen to their . . .?' Also the form of the question regularly indicates what to think, e.g. 'Do you really believe that . . .?', or 'So you think it's alright for him to turn round to me and say . . .?' Tone of voice and other paralinguistics are often crucial. Try putting first incredulity and then delight-at-insight into: 'You're telling me it could go either way?'

In the case of predisposing questions it is more honest to present the 'fact' or opinion without the interrogative form. Real questioning is too important to intellectual quest for us to permit such contamination. My belief is that these predisposing tendencies are so deep in us that we cannot eradicate them. So my regular strategy, as I indicate elsewhere, is to use the same features in a loaded question whose loaded content I do not hold. My deliberate mistake is intended to disorientate the child from the props and cues for the 'right' answer. I intend that this inoculation gives them courage when I unwittingly do the same thing for my treasured beliefs, as it does. I often debrief so that all children are clear. (I don't want them telling parents that Mr Quinn said: 'But girls shouldn't shift furniture. Should they?')

In my view, schooling has not sufficiently drawn attention to these aspects of human maturity. Neither has our other cultural influence. It is understandable that they should not; if these qualities were strengthened and deepened in people, the exercise and the abuse of power would be very much more difficult. Plato saw this clearly, and had the courage, in *The Republic*, not to conceal what the education of workers was based on. There are many 'Neo-Platonist' societies. If ours is to aspire to enhance autonomy, I offer a strategy to raise consciousness for the task.

The method of developing the virtues that follows is, through to adult level, good fun and harmlessly negative. I divide the class into small groups. To each group I give a secret note identifying an intellectual vice, which they portray in a three-minute improvisation. The entire class then guess at each vice. Of course, portrayed vices overlap, since one group, in ignorance of another's brief, cannot maintain boundaries. The vices are good-humouredly registered; indeed, by being often overdone, their viciousness is made more conspicuous and more awful. Reference back is then easier, retaining the qualities of vice and contempt – for the offence rather than the offender, if handled well. A word of warning about being overdone: experience has taught me that if the children play it for farce, they have much more fun, but at the expense of the important learning. So I urge them in advance that they are to make it as much like a real conversation as they can. I also say that there will be no applause after each presentation.

Each teacher identifies the most relevant vices for the class. I would often identify: frequent interrupting; one excluded; one making no effort or not responding to invitations; loaded questioning; body language/seating that excludes one; mere anecdotes talked past each other, each coming back to his own concern; one dominant 'boy(?)'; repetitive or overly long point-making; ridicule of opposed view. I introduce the vices as relevant to peer interaction rather than to that between child and teacher. It's wise to start with peer interaction, especially by a teacher who may lack confidence to deal with his own failings. But it must not end there, in an open community of enquiry. Despite protestations of ignorance, Plato's own practice of Socratic dialogue was as lordly as was his education theory. Our republics *and* our academies need fresh intellectual vigilance and fresh intellectual virtue from those in power.

Postscript

Stating virtue has no connection with claiming virtue. Even correct statement entails nothing about possession. A ubiquitous role of human being, we see when we look at others, is that of monumental mason of self-deception.

Chapter 10

Visualising problems and solutions

As with most things in schools apart from the sense-specific arts, thinking has had a predominance of the verbal. The visual has been underused. This is wrong in two ways. It is unfair to that group of children who are predominantly visualisers, who thrive in the visual medium. It is also wrong from the point of view of the topics. Just as some children are clearly visualisers, some problems are properly visual in the sense that both the problem and the solution are visual and are therefore best treated visually. We recognise this with maps in geography, with graphs in maths and so on, but it has been badly neglected in teaching thinking until recently.

The change has been the development, largely American, of visual organisers and thinking maps. These are designed not so much to communicate ideas, as graphs, designs and maps do, but to work out the ideas, to express them. For that reason, the pages representing work-sheets may appear too cluttered. In fact they are designed for groups of children who are clear what the task is: this is just the instrument of its completion. How the work is finally communicated to outsiders is a different, though important, matter.

Decision making is clearly an important skill to be developed. Figure 10.1 shows how children might be helped to go about it. It is a thinking map. Its use is to direct the children to a number of questions, a consideration of which will give them a better understanding of the skill and of how to approach it. The items on it are of course provisional and negotiable. I have drawn it from the Swartz and Parks book, but have added for example the 'desirable' questions to Swartz's five-question list. On this addition Swartz disagrees with me, as you are invited to. These lists gain real value when the children see that they are negotiable, and when they have criteria with which to negotiate. Undoubtedly, the best way to develop confidence is to use

SKILFUL DECISION MAKING

1. Is a decision necessary?

2. If not, is it desirable?

3. Why is it desirable?

4. What are my/our options?

5. What would the likely consequences be of each option?

6 How important, for or against, is each consequence?

7. Which option should I/we decide on?

Figure 10.1 Skilful decision making I (adapted from Swartz and Parks 1994)

the list a few times, with increasing complexity of material, and with shared consideration of its value. My favourite offering was from an eleven-year-old girl who said: 'All the questions ask for meta-thinking, but there isn't one that asks you to meta-think about decision making, *after* you have decided and seen the real consequences.'

Figure 10.1 is to be seen alongside Figure 10.2, which is a visual organiser. This allows the children to express their developing understanding of the particular point they are deciding. It does this better than continuous prose, as it gives an overview of their achievement and as they can easily home in on the stage in the process that they want to reconsider. It takes a very short time for children to become familiar with the routine of this structure, so that all their attention is given to the point of it.

Figure 10.3 shows another visual organiser, perhaps for a later stage in the sequence of deciding. Space is now available to represent visually the advantages and disadvantages of a particular option, leading to a strengthened choice, but still with scope to consider quality.

There is no shortage, across the National Curriculum and across children's lives, of opportunities to strengthen and avail oneself of this skill. Stories of course are a wonderful source. As I have argued, as soon as a story is stopped, and children are invited to think, the thoughts are in abundance. Decisions then are not far off. What could Bernard (in *Not Now, Bernard*) have done to get through to his parents? Beyond stories, we can ask: What might you do if you got separated from your dad in a town centre? What plants could you produce to sell for school funds?

I don't treat problem-solving separately from decision making here. The similarities are great, and visually organising problem-solving is very similar, in the layout of options and in judging them. The weaknesses of our and children's solving problems resemble the weaknesses of deciding, until we have worked on them: problems not recognised as problems; too few options considered; hasty solutions before considering consequences, and so forth.

The Swartz and Parks book has a number of worked examples, and I give two here (Figures 10.4 and 10.5) to show how the organiser was worked on these occasions. The story is the well-known one of Fern's horror at the plan of her father, Mr Arable, to axe the runt pig, from the beginning of E. B. White's *Charlotte's Web*. Remembering my earlier point that these are intended to express rather than communicate, it is still easy to see the value, to the group who have been through the process, of the lay-out, the visible markings, the oval highlighting of what is very important etc.

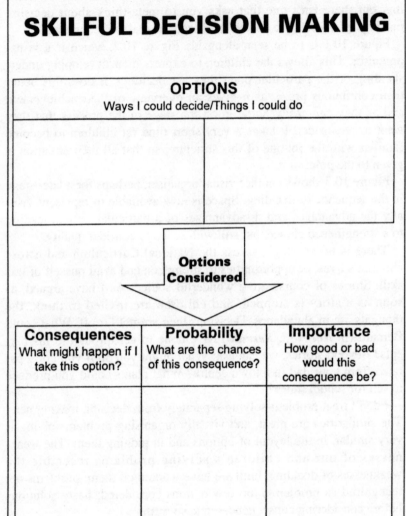

Figure 10.2 Skilful decision making II (adapted from Swartz and Parks 1994)

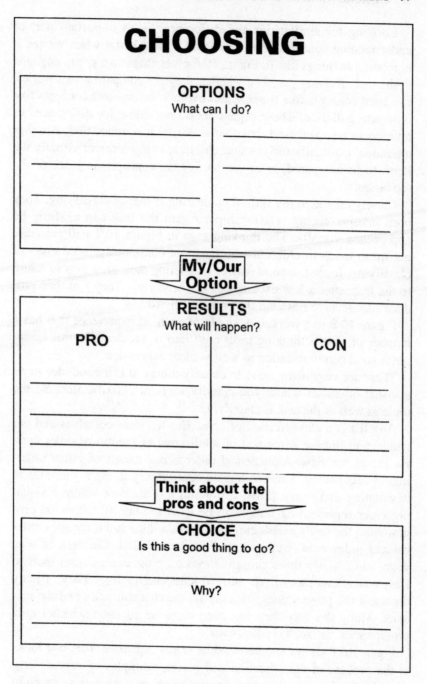

Figure 10.3 Choosing (adapted from Swartz and Parks 1994)

Looking for similarities and differences is an important part of understanding concepts. We understand a thing better when we see it in relation to things like it. Figure 10.6 gives shape to a group engaged in the task of doing just this, whether they are comparing two stories, two hard concepts like triangle and pyramid or two soft concepts like litter and pollution. These organisers do not allow for differences of opinion to be expressed, but that is easily accommodated. Another alteration, especially for younger children, is to represent visually the items to be compared, as an outline for the concepts, in place of the top boxes.

Closely related to the skill of comparing is that of classifying. They both involve seeing relationships. Again the task can usefully be approached visually. The thinking map in Figure 10.7 will probably not mean much to children who have not consciously faced tasks of classifying. Indeed, a good way of registering their growth is to return to the map after a few experiences of classifying. They can then produce anecdotes to flesh out the problems listed.

Figure 10.8 is a worked example of such an experience that has a number of simple thinking tasks built into it. Incidentally, this example is good communication as well as clear expression.

There are very many ways to classify things. It is a good idea to do a visual organiser where you classify ways of classification. So the topic as well as the task is classifying.

Any list is a classification of sorts. But we want ourselves and our children to impose some sort of intellectual or emotional order upon the things we view. Alphabetical order is one means of visual ordering, of sequencing, a means hugely contributory in eight-year-olds to developing dictionary skills. Chronology is another, where a visual organiser representing a day can be used to classify television programmes, the day's events etc. Ranking is a third and it requires criteria and judgement. But it should not be avoided. Children of nine years can classify three chosen television programmes from most to least educational, and from most to least entertaining. They visually represent the programmes, the criteria, the characteristics and the reasons. Along the way they can even come to question whether quiz programmes are 'really' educational.

Figure 10.9 shows another kind of visual organiser. This one looks at the process of classification and places examples of very diverse sets of animals under an organising set of criteria. As with so much in this chapter and elsewhere, the deepest value of the work is attained when the children are sufficiently familiar with it to devise a new set

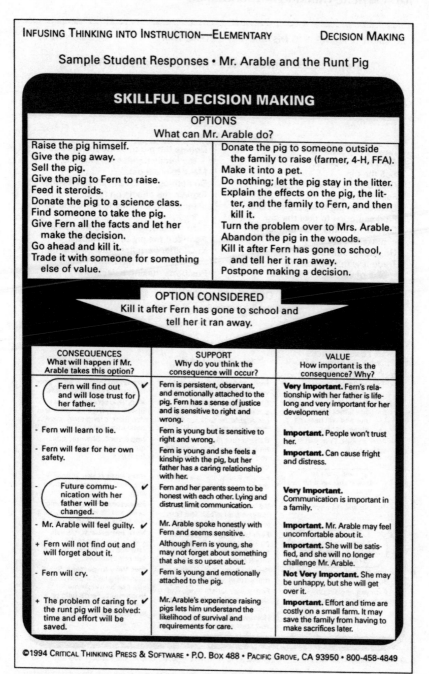

Sample Student Responses • Mr. Arable and the Runt Pig

SKILLFUL DECISION MAKING

OPTIONS
What can Mr. Arable do?

Raise the pig himself. Give the pig away. Sell the pig. Give the pig to Fern to raise. Feed it steroids. Donate the pig to a science class. Find someone to take the pig. Give Fern all the facts and let her make the decision. Go ahead and kill it. Trade it with someone for something else of value.	Donate the pig to someone outside the family to raise (farmer, 4-H, FFA). Make it into a pet. Do nothing; let the pig stay in the litter. Explain the effects on the pig, the litter, and the family to Fern, and then kill it. Turn the problem over to Mrs. Arable. Abandon the pig in the woods. Kill it after Fern has gone to school, and tell her it ran away. Postpone making a decision.

OPTION CONSIDERED
Kill it after Fern has gone to school and tell her it ran away.

CONSEQUENCES What will happen if Mr. Arable takes this option?	SUPPORT Why do you think the consequence will occur?	VALUE How important is the consequence? Why?
- Fern will find out and will lose trust for her father. ✔	Fern is persistent, observant, and emotionally attached to the pig. Fern has a sense of justice and is sensitive to right and wrong.	**Very Important.** Fern's relationship with her father is lifelong and very important for her development
- Fern will learn to lie.	Fern is young but is sensitive to right and wrong.	**Important.** People won't trust her.
- Fern will fear for her own safety.	Fern is young and she feels a kinship with the pig, but her father has a caring relationship with her.	**Important.** Can cause fright and distress.
- Future communication with her father will be changed. ✔	Fern and her parents seem to be honest with each other. Lying and distrust limit communication.	**Very Important.** Communication is important in a family.
- Mr. Arable will feel guilty. ✔	Mr. Arable spoke honestly with Fern and seems sensitive.	**Important.** Mr. Arable may feel uncomfortable about it.
+ Fern will not find out and will forget about it.	Although Fern is young, she may not forget about something that she is so upset about.	**Important.** She will be satisfied, and she will no longer challenge Mr. Arable.
- Fern will cry. ✔	Fern is young and emotionally attached to the pig.	**Not Very Important.** She may be unhappy, but she will get over it.
+ The problem of caring for the runt pig will be solved: time and effort will be saved. ✔	Mr. Arable's experience raising pigs lets him understand the likelihood of survival and requirements for care.	**Important.** Effort and time are costly on a small farm. It may save the family from having to make sacrifices later.

Figure 10.4 Sample student responses I (Swartz and Parks 1994)

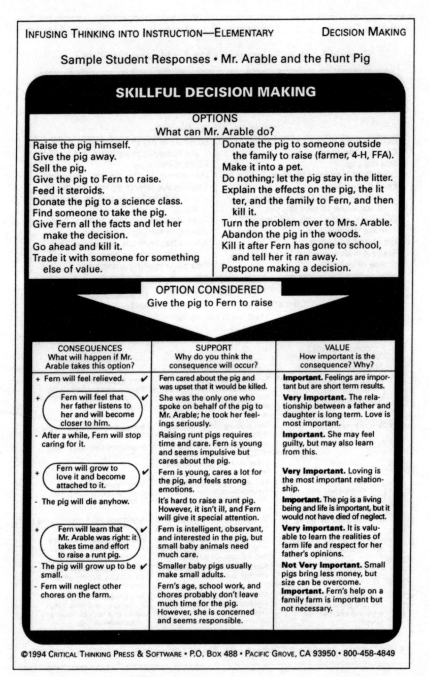

Sample Student Responses • Mr. Arable and the Runt Pig

SKILLFUL DECISION MAKING

OPTIONS
What can Mr. Arable do?

Raise the pig himself.	Donate the pig to someone outside
Give the pig away.	the family to raise (farmer, 4-H, FFA).
Sell the pig.	Make it into a pet.
Give the pig to Fern to raise.	Do nothing; let the pig stay in the litter.
Feed it steroids.	Explain the effects on the pig, the lit
Donate the pig to a science class.	ter, and the family to Fern, and then
Find someone to take the pig.	kill it.
Give Fern all the facts and let her	Turn the problem over to Mrs. Arable.
make the decision.	Abandon the pig in the woods.
Go ahead and kill it.	Kill it after Fern has gone to school,
Trade it with someone for something	and tell her it ran away.
else of value.	Postpone making a decision.

OPTION CONSIDERED
Give the pig to Fern to raise

CONSEQUENCES What will happen if Mr. Arable takes this option?	SUPPORT Why do you think the consequence will occur?	VALUE How important is the consequence? Why?
+ Fern will feel relieved. ✔	Fern cared about the pig and was upset that it would be killed.	**Important.** Feelings are important but are short term results.
+ Fern will feel that her father listens to her and will become closer to him. ✔	She was the only one who spoke on behalf of the pig to Mr. Arable; he took her feelings seriously.	**Very Important.** The relationship between a father and daughter is long term. Love is most important.
- After a while, Fern will stop caring for it.	Raising runt pigs requires time and care. Fern is young and seems impulsive but cares about the pig.	**Important.** She may feel guilty, but may also learn from this.
+ Fern will grow to love it and become attached to it. ✔	Fern is young, cares a lot for the pig, and feels strong emotions.	**Very Important.** Loving is the most important relationship.
- The pig will die anyhow.	It's hard to raise a runt pig. However, it isn't ill, and Fern will give it special attention.	**Important.** The pig is a living being and life is important, but it would not have died of neglect.
+ Fern will learn that Mr. Arable was right: it takes time and effort to raise a runt pig. ✔	Fern is intelligent, observant, and interested in the pig, but small baby animals need much care.	**Very important.** It is valuable to learn the realities of farm life and respect for her father's opinions.
- The pig will grow up to be small. ✔	Smaller baby pigs usually make small adults.	**Not Very Important.** Small pigs bring less money, but size can be overcome.
- Fern will neglect other chores on the farm.	Fern's age, school work, and chores probably don't leave much time for the pig. However, she is concerned and seems responsible.	**Important.** Fern's help on a family farm is important but not necessary.

Figure 10.5 Sample student responses II (Swartz and Parks 1994)

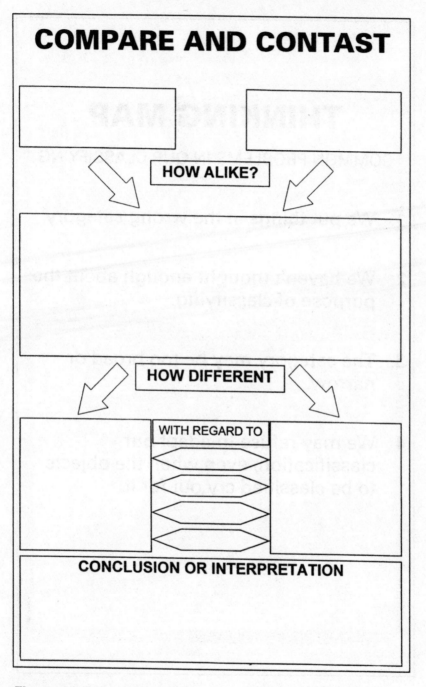

Figure 10.6 Compare and contrast (adapted from Swartz and Parks 1994)

THINKING MAP

COMMON PROBLEMS IN OUR CLASSIFYING

1. We put things in the wrong category.

2. We haven't thought enough about the purpose of classifying.

3. The category may be too broad or narrow.

4   We may refuse to adapt our classification, even when the objects to be classified cry out for it.

Figure 10.7 Thinking map (adapted from Swartz and Parks 1994)

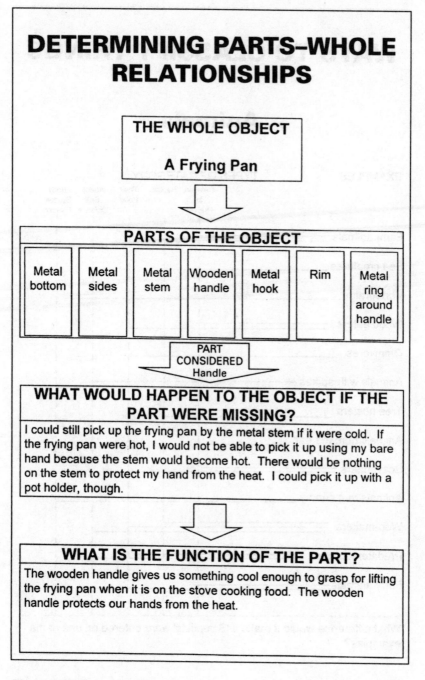

DETERMINING PARTS–WHOLE RELATIONSHIPS

THE WHOLE OBJECT

A Frying Pan

PARTS OF THE OBJECT

Metal bottom	Metal sides	Metal stem	Wooden handle	Metal hook	Rim	Metal ring around handle

PART CONSIDERED
Handle

WHAT WOULD HAPPEN TO THE OBJECT IF THE PART WERE MISSING?

I could still pick up the frying pan by the metal stem if it were cold. If the frying pan were hot, I would not be able to pick it up using my bare hand because the stem would become hot. There would be nothing on the stem to protect my hand from the heat. I could pick it up with a pot holder, though.

WHAT IS THE FUNCTION OF THE PART?

The wooden handle gives us something cool enough to grasp for lifting the frying pan when it is on the stove cooking food. The wooden handle protects our hands from the heat.

Figure 10.8 Determining parts–whole relationships (Swartz and Parks 1994)

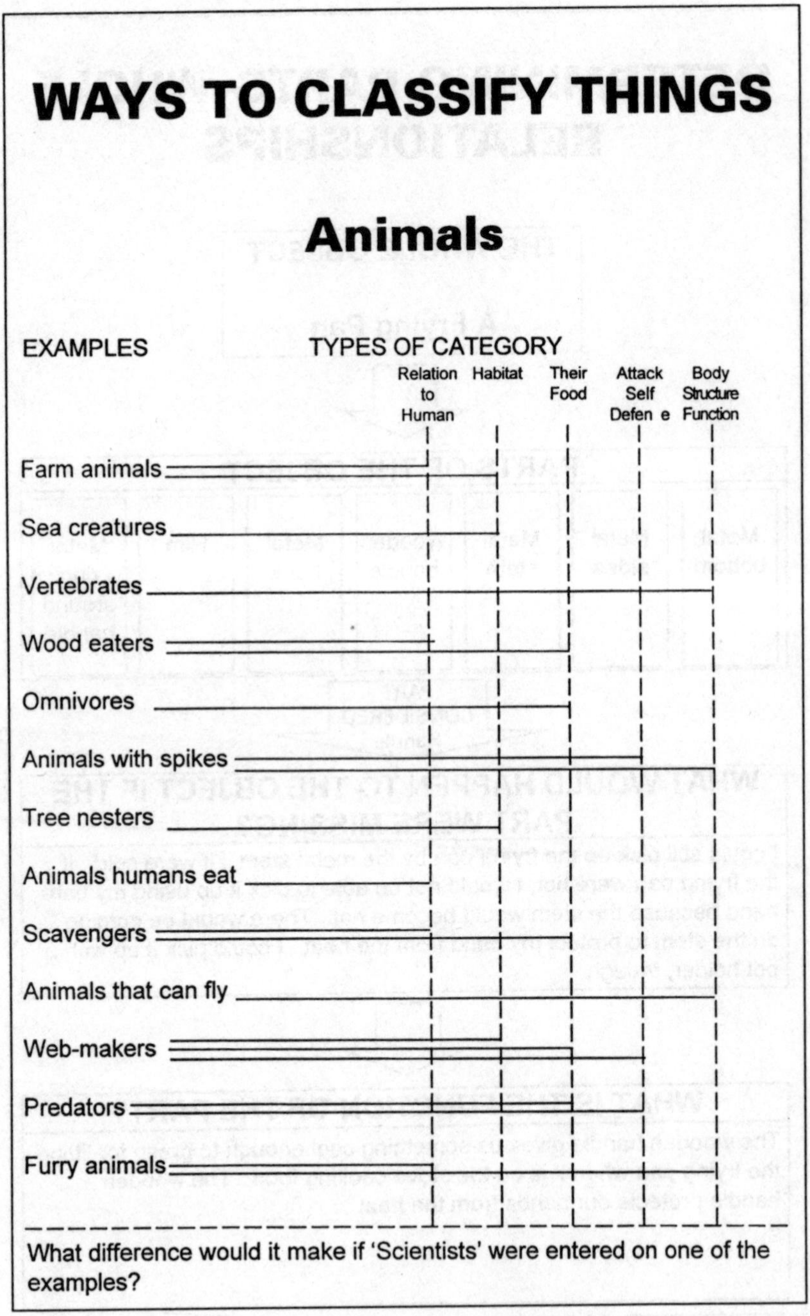

WAYS TO CLASSIFY THINGS

Animals

EXAMPLES   TYPES OF CATEGORY

	Relation to Human	Habitat	Their Food	Attack Self Defen e	Body Structure Function
Farm animals					
Sea creatures					
Vertebrates					
Wood eaters					
Omnivores					
Animals with spikes					
Tree nesters					
Animals humans eat					
Scavengers					
Animals that can fly					
Web-makers					
Predators					
Furry animals					

What difference would it make if 'Scientists' were entered on one of the examples?

Figure 10.9 Ways to classify things (adapted from Swartz and Parks 1994)

of animal sets and a new set of criteria. That achievement both demonstrates and develops ownership.

The same structure of visual organiser as that in Figure 10.9 is useful for another important purpose in critical thinking, questioning the reliability of sources. If you read to a class a factual claim about an observation or event, and ask them to list the questions they would want answered before they could assent to the claim, their questions will tend to fall into four categories. These categories can head the vertical dotted lines as in Figure 10.10, and the matching horizontal lines can be drawn from the questions listed on the left. This has the great value of helping children see the pattern of questioning that has general application, though even here I am keen for them to try to construct alternatives. In fact I defy them to!

I saw this approach to sources used to wonderful effect by Robert Swartz in teaching a class in his National Center for Teaching Thinking, in Boston. The class of adults heard the English folktale *Henny Penny* (alias *Chicken Licken*) in which Henny Penny feels the sky fall on her head, promptly tells Cocky Locky, Turkey Lurkey and the whole gang who are off to tell the king of this danger, until they also tell Foxey Loxey. The class were asked to think in groups about a number of questions. What I got from this was the identification of two kinds of defective thinking: 'Henny Penny' thinking and 'Cocky Locky' thinking. The former is jumping to a conclusion without a reasonable examination of the evidence. The latter is believing something on the basis of an unconfirmed report. Fiction is a great source of this critical learning, but what is so satisfying is to hear children use these terms in discussion to characterise non-fiction responses of others. The terms are useful labels, with humorous dismissal built into them. They are extremely important in preparing children for media reports. Figure 10.10 is not really necessary for the Henny Penny learning, as it is designed for reflection on non-fiction reports, but the categories of question can well be learned there.

Reasons and conclusions can usefully be represented visually, so that they stand apart from each other, but with their relationship on show. Figure 10.11 shows one such relationship, in one-sided reasoning, on a topic of wide educational interest. It can be modified in many ways, for example by incorporating the logically crucial words 'because', 'since', 'for', 'so', and 'therefore'.

QUESTIONS ABOUT THE RELIABILITY OF A SOURCE OF INFORMATION

QUESTIONS	TYPES OF QUESTIONS			
	Observer	Report	Conduct of Observation	Other Support

Figure 10.10 Questions about the reliability of a source of information (adapted from Swartz and Parks 1994)

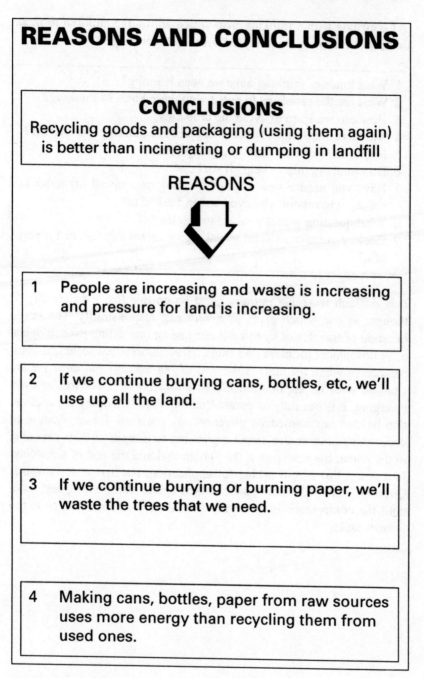

Figure 10.11 Reasons and conclusions (adapted from Swartz and Parks 1994)

I conclude with a thinking map which allows the children to meta-think about learning thinking and visually organising:

---

1 What kinds of thinking have we been learning?
2 What are the problems to avoid with these kinds of thinking?
3 How can we learn to avoid the problems?
4 Are there similarities between one kind of thinking and another?
5 Is it better/worse to work in a group? How?
6 Do visual organisers help? If so, how?
7 Have you used a new kind of thinking or a visual organiser at home, or in school when you weren't asked to?
8 What question would you add to this list?
9 Could you make a useful visual organiser for this list, or for part of it?

It is difficult to single out any question on this list. I do identify 7, though, as one which gives us a very real responsibility. The vexed question of transfer of learning is not just an interesting psychological or philosophical problem. We must never assume that technical competence in whatever skill is the end of our educational aim. We are charged with its application. So as competence is shown, or even emerging, it is our duty to ensure that the child is looking for application beyond our immediate direction. We must ask for application of decision making and/or visual organising to a topic of their choosing in the home, the newspaper, the playground and the rest of schooling. In a sense, this is still asking for application, but it is a step towards Question 7 above, which must be asked again, along with Question 6, until the competence is as readily available, where needed, as is the 5-times table.

Chapter 11

A quarrel and four arguments

Children are often told at home and school to stop arguing. This is wise advice, badly worded. What is meant is that they should stop quarrelling. But because they have not been taught the difference between arguing and quarrelling, how to argue well, and what kinds of argument there are, they easily slip unnoticing into the quarrel. I deal here with the four central kinds, and how to resolve them. In general, I find it best to allow children to argue without prior awareness of the difference; I introduce difference as they progress.

1 Empirical arguments

These are about matters of fact, observable, surveyable. In my science lesson, this was to the fore when we disagreed about the water rising in the bottle. I wrongly used argument from (empirical) authority, when (empirical) observation was the obviously intelligent way to proceed. I wanted them to articulate the supremacy and radical status of sensory observation over authority claims.

2 Conceptual arguments

These are about what words mean, about how concepts relate. It is possible within half an hour's work to have almost all of a class of nine-year-olds able to solve problems as to how two-concept sets relate to each other in the four possible relationships. This learning is only achieved if the logical effort is aided by the psychologically powerful device of Venn diagrams. But the achievement is a full one in accordance with my strict criterion that the children can not just solve

the range of problems, but can invent fresh, semantically complex
ones like: animals/people; trick/magic; lies/falsehoods; art/craft.

If this capacity is effectively taught, in technique and application,
there is little that could more profoundly influence the quality of argument among upper juniors. They learn quickly the regular error of the
question 'Which one is right?' And they learn the error of many adults
who reject distinctions because they unreflectingly use the model of
mutual exclusion as a universal feature of distinction. I have dealt with
this more technically, including the box I use for question (above the
centre line), and answer (below the line) in Quinn 1994a. The basic
question that is being asked is not 'Do P and A have anything in common?' but 'Are there members of either set A or set P that are not
members of the other set? Note that the answer is not given because
there is not just one right answer.

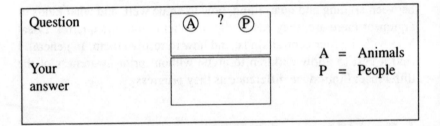

Figure 11.1 Box for question and answer (Quinn 1994a)

I approach the above complex box by giving children a clear understanding of what the box looks like with very simple, unambiguous
concepts as follows:

dog/horse	(mutual exclusion)	separate circles
dog/animal	(total inclusion)	one circle inside other
dog/black thing	(part inclusion)	circles overlap
dog/canine	(identity)	two circles are one

These four examples make the exercise sound trivial, as indeed it
should be. Children are here learning syntax of a method, so the
semantics should not also be a problem. When the method is learnt,
they are ready to avail themselves of it where the semantic relationship is the problem.

On the other hand, if the above four categories were very simple for
you, don't think they will be for all children or indeed adults. Of

course my preferred method is to pose the work as four problems, composing the boxes for question and answer. The initial diversity of response surprised me, but the process of negotiating agreement is a most useful one. As a teaching matter, I find it very useful to use the box layout, which to my knowledge is unique to me. The reason is that it allows me to zoom round the class often checking the answer from upside down. Another teaching point is that it is useful to number the four possibilities, to allow easy reference to the contrast between one's own and another's solution. (For example 'I think it is four rather than two because I can't think of any As that are not Bs.') This requires that the four types be illustrated in the room in accordance with Figure 11.2.

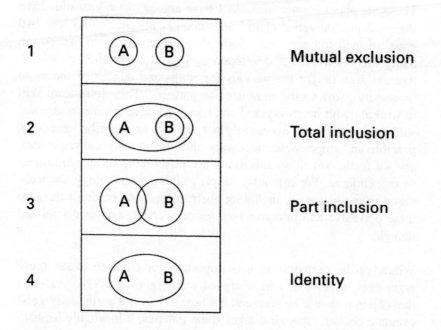

Figure 11.2 Venn diagram

3 Evaluative arguments

These are about attitudes and judgements, based on beauty, goodness, etc. Moral ones rise from our concern with the needs and interests of others as constraining our actions, e.g., 'Is it ever right to break a promise?' Five-year-olds largely think not. I tell them a story of two children who have promised faithfully to be home by six but, at five to six, see a baby drowning: 'Should they save the baby, or keep their promise?' They are easily manipulated into universal contradiction, as I word the question differently, but after ten minutes of my 'manipulation' are developing moral co-ordinates and are sticking more and more to their intellectual guns. In aesthetic areas, I am surprised at how few genuinely evaluative arguments or questions are raised with children about their own work or that of others.

4 Logical arguments

These are about connections. As I have argued, three-year-olds have the concepts 'universal claim' and 'counter instance': they say 'All gone' of their toy cars, and 'Some there' (pointing to an exception). Sadly this ability is not developed by logical exploration in school. Are children taught the various meanings and dances of the word 'necessary', with its different dancing partners? They don't learn skill in working with necessary and contingent connections; necessary and sufficient conditions; necessarily not and not necessarily; necessary, possible and impossible; necessary and unnecessary consequences, and so forth. Yet these intuitions are observable in any argument among children. We copiously supply training, terminology and technique in mathematics, including abstruse matter, but don't develop these pervasive and intrusive features of everyday and of disciplined thought.

Whatever the preparation, it is important for children to see these arguments in context. I have argued with eight- to twelve-year-olds that children should be seen and not heard. This is a particularly good example because, though it takes some minutes, it inevitably leads to the perception by the children of contradiction on my part: 'How can you say that, if you listen to what we say when we disagree with you?' Though I introduce little formal argument from logic, I do at times like to have them re-word this to reveal the basic logical structure which might be:

If you say 'Children should not be heard',
and if you listen carefully to what we say,
then you are contradicting yourself.
So you must be wrong either in what you say or what you do.

The failure to teach these and other features of argument is that we produce, in Britain at any rate, a population of school-leavers who get the popular press that we have earned for them, the level of parliamentary and media abuse that the purveyors of this abuse (market-sensitive souls if ever there were such) clearly judge they appreciate, and a standard of debate on public issues that is tragically laughable. One speaker on the BBC's 'serious' discussion programme *The Moral Maze* referred to another's 'tiny mind'. The second replied that the only things of his that were smaller than the first's were his nose and his liver. In ways I prefer the popular press: its pretensions are less culpable. But the fault lies still with us, the teachers, at least by omission, until such time as we attempt to establish rationality.

NC is a distinct disappointment on argument. The higher status of speaking and listening I have welcomed, but whereas Standard English is pervasively present, argument is scarcely mentioned, and the idea of learning constructive disagreement with a teacher, not at all. So far has NC failed to consider the field that it actually uses 'argumentative' where 'argumentational' is meant. Whereas I want to develop skill in argumentation, precisely what I want to diminish is the argumentativeness of children and adults.

So the failure to teach argument leads to the proliferation of quarrelling, where the goal of personal supremacy, not of improving beliefs, is what drives the effort. Self-aggrandisement is a powerful and dazzling distraction from the pursuit of truth, and when controversy in reasoning becomes quarrelling, we seek to do the other down by whatever means come to mind. It seems as though we only hold on to the argument to the extent that to leave it altogether might seem foolish. At times we do let go, and the exchange then acquires at least the honesty it previously lacked, as fists, curses, etc fly. There is then no blurring of the distinction between argument proper and quarrel. This is an extreme failure of decentring.

The advice 'Stop arguing' becomes 'Try arguing instead'. But education in argument is necessary for the advice to make sense.

Chapter 12

Climate and pedagogy

Ideally, as a chapter, this would be redundant, since it would be so clear in all chapters. Here, I spell it out.

1 **Humour** is more important than can be put into words. If I did not have the children laugh with me about every ten minutes, I could not achieve what I attempt, especially in the extended periods of deep speaking and listening that I find so useful. All can instantly be captivated by a great laugh together. The power of classroom laughter is frightening; its avoidance by so many teachers frightens me. As I have often argued, its value is not just relief, but the closeness and togetherness it brings to the relationship of teacher and child.

2 **Provocation-in-role** is the technique I most often use to achieve humour and is the feature for which I am most criticised. When I have better ways of enchanting and challenging children, I use them.

   But the technique is not just for humour. I have argued (Quinn 1994b) the importance of children learning to stand up for themselves, to resist especially undue pressure. They must identify what is provocative in what adults say to them and develop confidence to counter such edginess, not by matching irritation and aggression, but by reason and argument proper. My use of provocation, abuse, derision etc is to *undermine* their value. My main means of doing so is by being offensively in the wrong, and having my error identified publicly. Children love it, and still somehow seem to love me! But other teachers have other techniques that work well for them, to achieve both humour and autonomy.

3 **Listening** is a non-negotiable skill of an educator, though you can teach without it. Children sense when you want to know and attend

to what they think and feel. They are often astonished to discover that the teacher really does want to know. Schooling, as they often put it to me, is not about that. What they are listening for, as I said earlier, is a clue as to what is the 'right', expected answer. I think it is true that none of us know how true this is of our teaching. I am taken aback when I attend to recordings. To allow for this, I use the previous strategy, so that I systematically disorientate the children as to what the teacher's desired answer is. My paralanguage disorientates them. I get them to know that they cannot rely on my clues, that it is their real views I want to hear.

4 **Challenge** is a crucial feature of an educative classroom. Clearly, the challenge has to take account of the confidence resource of the children. With children I don't know well, humour allows me to go further than I otherwise could. But the climate of the classroom must challenge their ideas, their beliefs, their attitudes, their aspirations. Children must learn that the challenge should come from them as much as from the teacher. And they must develop the important skills of giving and receiving criticism, the life-blood of challenge.

5 **Intelligence** is a climate factor often missing from classrooms. Earlier, I used the contrast between academic and intellectual; teachers often have too high academic expectations of children at the same time and in the same activities as those in which they have too low intellectual expectations. Sadly, teachers and OFSTED inspectors often do not distinguish these, using 'academic' for both. They thereby fail to make a distinction that goes to the heart of the difference between classrooms that do, and those that do not, celebrate intelligence. The difference is this: the academic has to do with the conventions, the routines of a subject; the intellectual has to do with the exercise, development, exploration, and articulation of intelligence. We need the latter for its own sake and for its contribution to the former. We could do with more intellectual academics, not just trained ones.

6 **Pedagogy for judgement.** For some lucky children, a single exposure to the music of the 'cello, to horseriding, to general or specific tasks in technology or to a maths skill is sufficient for them to grasp the significance as a whole and to be able to decide educatedly about it. With most techniques in CT, as in most areas of skill, a number of exposures are necessary to develop the skill, to learn its value and to appreciate the range of its application. The Venn

diagram is an example I have given of a skill I have taught successfully in one short lesson. But my claim is more modest than it
seems. What I have taught is the basic skill, not its value and the
diversity of its application. As with pointillist painting, it takes for
nearly all children a number of lessons before they can not only use
it but both judge and be disposed to judge when it is appropriate to
use, beyond being prompted by the teacher.

But that is the criterion of success: being prompted appropriately
by the circumstances of the task, the engagement, the life – not the
teacher. Anything short of that criterion is, for most children, technical competence; training but not education. The pedagogic point
is not one of special pleading, quite the opposite: it is to see the
method of teaching/learning CT as in the mainstream of learning
educational skills. It is to see thinking skills as requiring repeated,
developmental practice before they become educational attain-
ments, that is before they become judgement or critical thinking.

7 **Common sense.** The antithesis of common sense and mystification
is a useful one in considering climate. Many children and adults
have been introduced to science and have been put off science,
because it was introduced as a series of mysteries to be remem-
bered, a set of academic store-pieces, for them to avail themselves
of, if they remember, on the occasion of certain prompts such as
exam questions or others' remarks. Science is often thus trivialised
and sterilised. The expression 'blinded with science' suggests a
more sinister power relationship based on misuse of mystery.

To avoid this sterility, it is necessary from the early stages that
science be rooted in children's common sense, that it be a development out of common sense, rather than a superimposition upon
existing understanding. My use of magic, then, is deliberately an
affront to common sense, rather than a bypass. Magic always works
thus, at least with children, so that their Piagetian disequilibration is
activated, their schemata are in turmoil. They anxiously seek a resolution that will allow their minds to rest, but crucially, from the educator's point of view, a resolution that will have a more generous
accommodation of the physical world, that will not be disequilibrat-
ed in future by evidence of hot air expanding. My educational
magic triggers not the trivial detection of a sleight of hand, but a
new feature in the regularity of the observable world. If the learning
is mere academic learning, and does not affect their commonsense
grasp of the world, my work is largely a failure.

The point is not particularly one about science; it applies to all subjects. It is not particularly about psychology of learning, though it applies there; it is an epistemological point about the nature and ontogenesis of understanding. Disciplines of meaning like science, philosophy and the arts came about in an evolutionary way as the outcome of struggle to make sense of the world. The human birthright is not just to encounter the sense that has been made of the world, but to encounter the world that is to be made sense of and the means of making sense. The child must be helped to extend her common sense by the growing realisation of the powers of observation, of criticism, of construction etc that are abundantly evident in the dynamic of disturbed common sense.

This groundwork should be evident in my work with the children, where their common sense making sense is triggered by my anti-empirical nonsense. I see this as a paradigm case of their seeing the emergence of the scientific spirit and method. I see it also as a paradigm case of A. N. Whitehead's brilliant prescription for education, detailed later, of the rhythm of education being romance, precision and generalisation. Romance and generalisation are the direct points of contact with common sense; in a well-handled education, precision never quite loses contact with, and is often vigorously infused with, common sense.

8 **Acceptance** is my final point about climate. Of course not everything that I hear in school is acceptable. But the children's and my challenge must be in a climate of listening, of 'hearing the best of' what is offered. So often, children are done down, as I was at school, because they venture, because they explore, because they imaginatively hypothesise, because they dare to create and think beyond the teacher's imagination or instigation. Challenge, acceptingly. The paradox of the unaccepting role I play serves to emphasise to children, as we laugh at my foolishness and as we debrief, how important the opposite disposition is, and how important it is to listen to the dismissive adult, to resist him, and to counter his dismissal.

Chapter 13

Some theoretical perspectives

The views I have expressed are hugely at variance with those endorsed by many philosophers of education. I quote, with brief comment, Dame Mary Warnock:

> Our first duty as teachers must be to teach what is known. And this carries with it the mark of non-relativity. One is saying 'this is how it was' or 'this is how it is'. One cannot consistently, in the same breath, say 'but it may not have been' or 'but I may be wrong'. To adopt any other method is to allow nothing in the curriculum except philosophy.
>
> (Warnock 1977, pp. 121–2)

Since I often am wrong, I must say: 'It may not have been' and 'I may be wrong'. If I am obliged to declare to children or academics, as I am, whether I may be wrong or not, I consistently say: 'Indeed, sadly, yes'. Warnock has access to something to which I do not, and from which my philosophy is excluded. She needs to indicate the criterion by which the space between subjective certainty or indeed intersubjective certainty, and objective truth, can be bridged. Such a bridge would support many teachers as well as causing a major revolution in the development of two and a half millennia of European philosophy. Plato and Kant should experience a major revival in their aspirations to determine objective, infallible truth, i.e., respectively, access to Platonic forms of objective reality, and access to the Kantian transcendental deduction of truths. To adopt a pedagogic constraint of fallibility, based on being often wrong, as I am, is to allow nothing in the curriculum that I cannot philosophically defend. Warnock refers, in an earlier passage, to fallibility, but as can be seen from the quotation, her curriculum recommendation is not constrained by teacher fallibility.

Professor R. S. Peters writes about subjects like

... arithmetic where rules have simply to be learnt defining what is right or wrong and where, in the early stages at any rate, there is little scope for rational explanation or learning by experience.

(Peters 1973, p. 129)

This seems like an empirical claim, so the empirical basis can be demanded. I prefer to object conceptually: if arithmetic rules have simply to be learnt in that way, then how did we chance on them in the first place? There is huge scope for rational explanation and learning by experience since the rules of arithmetic, unlike works of art, are human discoveries rather than inventions. Arithmetic learned otherwise is largely training, not education. Peters' view on arithmetic is even more objectionable in an area like science, where there is less scope for *a priori* truth. And yet he claims that 'Science is the supreme example of reason in action' for a variety of reasons, including that '... its testing procedures ... guarantee objectivity and the escape from arbitrariness'. (Peters 1974, pp. 154, 424). I respond: nothing that I can conceive of guarantees objectivity, and since I am in the company of most philosophers of science on the issue, I can leave the onus of proof on Peters.

In relation to scientific objectivity in my doctorate, Professor Sir Karl Popper, perhaps the twentieth century's most distinguished philosopher of science, advised me to contact his former student R. S. Peters. I hold with the master, not the student, when the master writes, about Gilbert Ryle's view that 'established' scientific theories are 'laws':

This view of Ryle's was indeed almost the established standard at the time I wrote [*The Logic of Scientific Enquiry*], and it is by no means dead. I first turned against it because of Einstein's theory of gravity: there never was a theory as well 'established' as Newton's, and it is unlikely that there ever will be one; but whatever one may think of the status of Einstein's theory, it certainly taught us to look at Newton's as a mere hypothesis or conjecture.

(Popper 1972, p. 9)

Popper puts the point less anecdotally, more formally, thus: ' ... no number of test statements would justify the claim that an explanatory universal theory is true' (p. 9).

Professor P. H. Hirst argues that

The provision of experience in itself is quite inadequate for developing even the simplest body of concepts, and without these nothing more complex can possibly be achieved.

(Hirst 1974, p. 24)

Again I use the conceptual objection: if experience strictly cannot develop concepts, whence concepts? Or in imagination, could not two children, brought up on a desert island without teaching and with only experience to learn from, develop the concepts 'rise', 'unfair', 'cold', 'bridging'?

These theorists overstate the role of teacher as transmitter; they undervalue the role of teacher as developer, as extractor, as questioner. They understate the potential of the child to learn by experience beyond Peters, to develop concepts beyond Hirst and to interrogate Warnock's 'knowns', her 'non-relativities'. If they are right, my efforts with children are confused, conceited and in vain.

A. N. Whitehead gave illuminating images, models and theories of good education. His retreat from 'inert ideas' leads to the advice that ideas in a child's education

> ... be thrown into every combination possible. The child should make them his own, and should understand their application here and now in the circumstances of his actual life. From the very beginning of his education, the child should experience the joy of discovery. The discovery which he has to make, is that general ideas give an understanding of that stream of events which pours through his life, which is his life.
>
> (Whitehead 1917, p. 3)

His model of the rhythm of education is usefully grounded in patterns of introduction, development and application. His most useful contribution is, I believe, in avoiding an exclusive concern with the second stage, what he calls 'precision'. Sadly, many of those, like Peters, who cannot resist the force of this model consider that the move from romance to precision is a one-off matter, and then the precision stage is a 'long hard slog', until generalisation dawns. They do not attend to Whitehead's urging that this rhythmic pattern should be evident in every course of study and in every lesson. It is a point about the intelligent absorption of subject matter as much as a point about the longitudinal development of the individual.

Perhaps Whitehead's fine quotation is an opportunity for me to correct an impression that my regular emphasis on 'the intellectual' might give. I have taken pains to emphasise the intellectual by contrast with the academic, but not with the affective. The connection I see between cognition and affection is so close that I do not value any cognitive achievement that is not seen by the achiever to rest on feelings. All values, including truth itself, exist in an important respect as response to our feeling needs, responses to the need for regularity (Popper

1972, p. 230), to the interrogation of common sense (Pring 1976), to intellectual Eros (Elliott 1975, p. 66) and to the joy of discovery (Whitehead 1917, p. 3).

Many authors dismiss the re-invention of the wheel. Such people attend more to the importance of wheels than of re-invention, they think more of re-invention than of education, and ignore the point that re-invention is just a form of invention, of creativity. Intellectual invention is not just the development of inventiveness; it is a process of hugely more pleasure than being told a truth, and is often an even greater pleasure when it is achieved against a Cartesian evil demon who is telling lies about air, heat, water, density and how children should learn.

Chapter 14

Quality assessment: quality display

Vocabulary extension immediately comes to mind when considering the development of thought, and so it should. With words being so central in the conduct and communication of thought, any increase in thought would normally lead to an increase in vocabulary. There is great scope for the practice of self-recording here, with the child taking responsibility for identifying a certain number of words each week that are new and specially interesting. If my concern is with concepts like contradiction, pressure or density, I must devise ways in which I can test their grasp of this new material. My preference is for a task which tests fresh application of the concept, and which tests whether the word is unselfconsciously part of the child's active vocabulary.

Whilst vocabulary comes readily to mind, there is a huge danger that it is accorded status beyond its worth. It is a conspicuous but often superficial feature of learning gain. As implied in the previous paragraph, we must also test for meaning gain. I prefer nearly always to establish the concept before the children hear the word. So they can say: a particular disagreement is 'that sort that you need to observe for', before they hear the word 'empirical'; 'the air is looking for more space', before hearing 'pressure'; 'we are thinking about thinking', before 'meta-thinking' is introduced. The testing reflects this concern. We test for the semantic vigour that comes of well-matched words and concepts which the child can relate, reverse, apply and so forth. One of the most exciting and encouraging things to a teacher new to this way of working is the depth of children's understanding of material learned largely under their own steam in community of enquiry, or in accordance with the criteria in the chapter 'Climate and Pedagogy'.

Along with the grasp of new meanings comes a concern to show how well the children have extended their grasp of syntax. The original NC served a good purpose in registering the importance of speech.

Logical connectives abound in children's speech. We should check and show that they can use, in increasingly complex structures, terms like 'unless', 'since', 'if . . . then', 'doesn't necessarily' and so on.

Those who want to ensure that there is conspicuous evidence of the work going on in speaking and listening can use a technique that has this as well as deeper virtues. There is an astonishing and little attended-to discrepancy between the strength of what children say and the weakness of what they write, particularly in non-fiction. With a new class, one can easily hear a host of spoken sentences, in science, philosophy or whatever, that the children could not conceivably have written. The logical syntax is deft and complex, and the subordinate clauses are appropriate. When the child's work is scribed, word-processed, re-drafted by the author and on display, it strikes the adult reader (OFSTED, head, advisor) as merely an exercise in dictation, until the author is questioned about the content. So there is scope not just to publicise the work, but to make significant inroads into thoughtful literacy, for the sake both of children whose writing is banal and of adults who are sceptical of 'mere talk' without evidence.

This strategy of scribing by peer or teacher is a useful addition to the more standard methods of audio and video recordings, which have a central place in speaking and listening. The written record on display can be hugely beneficial in prompting the children to think about syntactic freshness in their subsequent writing. I use in display children's reflections on their writing, alongside the writing, to abstract and highlight qualities such as sentences beginning with: 'But having not understood . . .', 'Although . . .', 'Whenever . . .', 'When I was thinking that . . .'.

An example can bring together the various points in this section, which has as much to do with aims as with assessment and recording. Meta-reflection is of profound importance in children's learning, and is therefore a proper object of assessment and recording. Consider the assessable qualities of the following, giving duly scant attention to the precocity of big words, attending rather to the conceptual and syntactic vigour of the passage, scribed by me (and re-drafted by the speaker) from a conversation of an eleven-year-old; consider too its value in display.

I think you're wrong [Mr Quinn] to say that it couldn't be called 'meta-questioning', because if meta-philosophy is called 'meta-philosophy' because it's philosophy about philosophy, then you could just take the meta bit and put it before the 'questioning', because it's questioning about questioning, and it's the same as meta-thinking, that you said, so it could be and even if it isn't it should be because of the way it fits. [Pause] In fact, since the question [are there any questions that there are not right answers to?] is the biggest question in the world, it's the mega-meta-question. [Pause] And if you ask me a question about it, it'll be a meta-mega-meta-question.

Bibliography

Abbs, P. (1993) *Socratic Education: Aspects of Education No. 49*, Hull, University of Hull.

Addy, P. and Shayer, M. (1994) *Really Raising Standards: Cognitive Intervention and Academic Achievement*, London, Routledge.

Baron, J. B. and Sternberg, R. J. (eds) (1987) *Teaching Thinking Skills: Theory and Practice*, New York, W. H. Freeman and Co.

Baumfield, V. (1995) *Improving Students' Performance: A Guide to Thinking Skills Programmes in Education and Training*, Gateshead, Tyneside TEC/Newcastle University.

Bonnett, M. (1994) *Children's Thinking*, London, Cassell.

Camhy, D. G. (ed.) (1994) *Children: Thinking and Philosophy* (Proceedings of the 5th International Conference of Philosophy for Children, Graz, 1992), Sankt Augustin, Austria, Academia Verlag.

Coles, M. J. and Robinson, W. D. (eds) (1991, Second Edition) *Teaching Thinking: A Survey of Programmes in Education*, Bristol, Bristol Classical Press.

Dingli, S. (ed) (1995) *Creative Thinking: A Multifaceted Approach*, Malta, University of Malta Press.

Elliott, R. K. (1975) 'Education and Human Being' in Brown, S. C. (ed.) *Philosophers Discuss Education*, London, Macmillan.

Ennis, R. H. (1996) *Critical Thinking*, Upper Saddle River, NJ, Prentice Hall.

Fisher, A. (1991) 'Effective Learning and the Critical Thinking Movement' in Coles and Robinson 1991.

Fisher, R. (1995) *Teaching Children to Learn*, Cheltenham, Stanley Thornes.

Fisher, R. (1996) *Stories for Thinking*, Wantage, Nash Pollock.

Fisher, R. (1997) *Games for Thinking*, Wantage, Nash Pollock.

Fox, R. (1996) *Thinking Matters: Stories to Encourage Thinking Skills*, Exmouth, Southgate.

Gaarder, J. (1995) *Sophie's World*, London, Phoenix House.

Gardner, P. and Johnson, S. (1996) 'Thinking Critically about Critical Thinking: an unskilled inquiry into Quinn and McPeck', *Journal of*

Philosophy of Education, 30, 3.

Hare, W. (1995) 'Content and Criticism: The Aims of Schooling', *Journal of Philosophy of Education*, 29, 1.

Hirst, P. H. (1974) *Knowledge and the Curriculum*, London, Routledge and Kegan Paul.

LeVine, R. A. and White, M. I. (1995) *Human Conditions: The Cultural Basis of Human Development*, New York, Routledge and Kegan Paul.

Lipman, M. (1988) *Philosophy Goes to School*, Philadelphia, Temple University Press.

Meno Project (1993) *Thinking Skills*, Cambridge, University of Cambridge LES.

Moore, B. and Parker, R. (1992) *Critical Thinking*, Mountain View, CA, Mayfield Publishing Company.

Murris, K. (1995) *Teaching Philosophy With Picture Books*, London, Infonet.

Peters, R. S. (1973, Third Edition) *Authority, Responsibility and Education*, London, Allen and Unwin.

Peters, R. S. (1974) *Psychology and Ethical Development*, London, Allen and Unwin.

Piaget, J. (1932) *The Moral Judgement of the Child*, London, Routledge and Kegan Paul.

Popper, K. (1972) *Objective Knowledge*, Oxford, Clarendon Press.

Pring, R. (1976) *Schools of Thought*, London, Open Books.

Quinn, V. (1994a) 'In Defence of Critical Thinking as a Subject: If McPeck is wrong, he is wrong', *Journal of Philosophy of Education*, 28, 1.

Quinn, V. (1994b) 'Provocation in Role', *Journal of SAPERE*, 8, 1.

Quinn, V. (1995a) 'Sarah's Growth in Contradiction: A case study of 7/8 year-olds starting logic', *Early Child Development and Care*, 107.

Quinn, V. (1995b) *Magic, Science and Critical Thinking: 'Sir, Can I Disagree With You?'*, Wakefield, Bretton Hall Philosophy and Critical Thinking Unit.

Smeyers, P. (1995) 'Education and the Educational Project 1: The Atmosphere of Post-Modernism', *Journal of Philosophy of Education*, 29, 1.

Splitter, L. (1994) 'Questioning as the Stimulus to Inquiry' in Camhy 1994.

Sutcliffe, R. (1993) (adapted from Lipman 1988) *Harry Stottlemeier's Discovery*, Horsham, SAPERE.

Swartz, R. J. and Parks, S. (1994) *Infusing the Teaching of Critical and Creative Thinking into Content Instruction*, Pacific Grove, CA, Critical Thinking Press and Software.

Walton, D. (1992) *The Place of Emotion in Argument*, Pennsylvania, Pennsylvania State University Press.

Warnock, M. (1977) *Schools of Thought*, London, Faber.

Whitehead, A. N. (1917) *The Aims of Education*, London, Williams and Norgate.

Wood, D. (1997, Second Edition) *How Children Think and Learn*, London, Blackwell.

Young, S. (1994) 'It Stands to Reason', *TES*, 29 April, 1–2.

If . . . then: The Journal of Philosophical Enquiry in Education is a useful account of current British work in the field. It is published by SAPERE. Details from R. Sutcliffe, Christ's Hospital, Horsham, Surrey.

Index